£10
1238

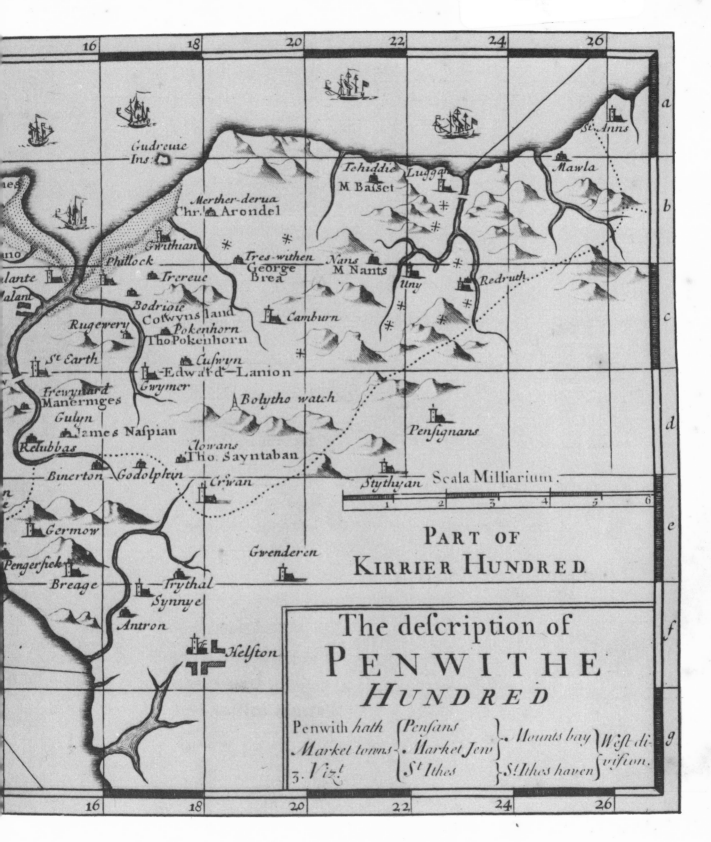

16 18 20 22 24 26

a

St Anns

Gudreue
Ins:

Mawla

b

Tehiddie
M Basset

Luggan

Merther-derua
Chr: Arondel

Gwithian

Tres-withen
George
Brea

Nans
M Nants

Redruth

c

Phillock

Trereue

Bodrioie
Cotwyns Iland
Pokenhorn
Tho Pokenhorn

Uny

Rugewery

Camburn

St Earth

Cuswyn
Edward Lanion

Frewynard
Manermges

Gwymer

Bolytho watch

d

Gulyn
James Naspian

Pensignans

Relubbas

Clowans
Tho Saytaban

Binerton Godolphin

Crwan

Stythyan Scala Milliarium.

e

Germow

Gwenderen

1 2 3 4 5 6

PART OF
KIRRIER HUNDRED.

Pengersick
Breage

Trythal
Synnye

f

Antron

Helston

The description of
PENWITHE
HUNDRED

Penwith hath
Market towns
3. Viz!

{ Pensans
Market Jew
St Ithes

} • Mounts bay
} • St Ithes haven

West di-
vision.

g

16 18 20 22 24 26

THE ILLUSTRATED PAST: PENWITH

FRONT COVER: Photographers at Land's End, 1903; Hughes, Burrow
and Thomas. (CCL)

'Henny' (Henry) Quick in 1833. (M)

THE ILLUSTRATED PAST:
PENWITH

AN HISTORICAL SURVEY OF THE LAND'S END DISTRICT

BY

CYRIL NOALL

BARRACUDA BOOKS LIMITED
BUCKINGHAM, ENGLAND
MCMLXXVIII

PUBLISHED BY BARRACUDA BOOKS LIMITED

BUCKINGHAM, ENGLAND

AND PRINTED BY

FRANK ROOK LIMITED

TOWER BRIDGE ROAD

LONDON SE1

BOUND BY

BOOKBINDERS OF LONDON LIMITED

LONDON N5

JACKET PRINTED BY

WHITE CRESCENT PRESS LIMITED

LUTON, ENGLAND

LITHOGRAPHY BY

SOUTH MIDLANDS LITHO PLATES LIMITED

LUTON, ENGLAND

DISPLAY TYPE SET IN

MONOTYPE BASKERVILLE SERIES 169

BY SOUTH BUCKS TYPESETTERS LIMITED

BEACONSFIELD, ENGLAND

TEXT SET IN 12/14PT BASKERVILLE

BY BEAVER REPROGRAPHICS LIMITED

BUSHEY, ENGLAND

© Cyril Noall 1978

ISBN 0 86023 047 3

Contents

Acknowledgements

It would be imposible to produce such a book as this without the generous support of many well-wishers who gladly made available cherished photographs from their own collections or helped with information and advice; I am most grateful to them all for their assistance.

With few exceptions, the photographs were either specially taken or copied by William Thomas. His skill in reviving faded or damaged prints and coping with difficult subjects can only be truly appreciated by those familiar with the originals, but the general high quality of his work will be apparent to all. I am also much indebted to him for practical help in other matters.

The two largest photographic collections drawn upon were those at Penlee House Museum (by courtesy of Penwith District Council and its Museums Officer, Mrs Gaynor Kavanagh) and at the Cornwall County Library Local Studies Department, Redruth (Terry Knight). Regalia and documents of the former Penzance Borough Council were photographed by courtesy of Arthur Berryman, Mayor of Penzance, and the Penzance Charter Trustees, and those of the former Borough of Marazion by permission of Marazion Town Trust and its Treasurer, Francis C. Hosking, CC.

Photographs were also provided by the following: Prof. Charles Thomas, MA, FSA, of the Institute of Cornish Studies, Pool, Redruth; J. M. Hosking, Tower Farm, St Buryan; W. E. Chapple, St Buryan; Alfred Olds, Tevorian Farm, Sancreed; David Thomas, BA, Camborne; Miss G. M. Bray, Camborne; Miss R. Mitchell, Camborne; the Misses G. and L. Bruford, Camborne; Alfred Eddy, Boleigh Farm, St Buryan; P. L. Hull, MA, County Archivist, and J. C. Edwards, County Record Office, Truro; Dick Matthews, Gulval; Miss S. J. Corin, Gulval; T. J. Matthews, Gulval; C. Tregonning, Gulval; E. W. A. Edmonds, Perranwell; Dr Hugh Hynes, Penzance; Stanley Cock (Secretary) and the Trustees of St Ives Museum; Studio St Ives Ltd, St Ives; Richards (Photographers) Penzance; H. L. Douch, BA, Curator, County Museum, Truro; S. Bennetts, St Ives; Percy Quick, St Ives; Brian Stevens, St Ives; the late Miss Dora R. Chirgwin and W. Chirgwin, St Just ; and the Devon County Record Office, Exeter.

Permission to photograph was given by the Rev F. W. Warnes, Vicar of Gulval; the Rev Charles Hutton, Rector of Ludgvan; the Rev Maurice Friggens, Rector of St Buryan; the Rev R. H. Cadman, Vicar of Paul; the Rev R. J. Mackenzie, Rector of Perranuthnoe; the Rev R. J. Elford, Rector of Phillack; the Rev G. R. Wells, Vicar of St Erth; the Rev William Rowett, Vicar of Madron; Canon J. B. D. Cotter, Vicar of Zennor; the Rev G. B. Whittaker, Vicar of Lelant; and the Rev David J. M. Jasper, Vicar of St Just.

I also wish to express my thanks to Bernard Hicks of Sennen, Chairman of Penwith District Council, who first suggested that this book should be written; the Penwith District Council and Cornwall County Library (County Librarian, John Farmer) for their support; the staff of St Ives Library; Mrs S. Balson, Librarian of Penzance (Morrab Gardens) Library; E. T. Berryman, Towednack; N. Kent, Public Record Office, London; D. J. Goddard, Map Library, the British Library; and Nelson Hosking, Boskennal Farm, St Buryan.

Foreword

by Councillor T.B. Hicks, Chairman of Penwith District Council

It is with the greatest of pleasure that I write the foreword to this book on Penwith. I should like to congratulate the author and publishers on taking the initiative to produce such a book on our area.

It shows how each settlement in the district originated, changed and became today's village and parish. The cultural activities, historic background and indigenous industries are all identified, in one form or another covering the whole district of Penwith.

The publication of this book is most opportune, in that the 1974 reorganisation brought the peninsula under the administration of one local authority. The rural area of West Penwith and the urban area of St Just, with the Boroughs of Penzance and St Ives, make up what is to me the finest piece of country to be found anywhere. The pictures are a delight, and as present Chairman of the Council I am honoured to be associated with this publication and wish all concerned every success.

T. B. Hicks

To The Land's End

The sunbeams tremble; and the purple light
Illumines the dark Bolerium, seat of Storms!
Drear are his granite wilds, his schistine rocks
Encircled by the wave, where to the gale
The haggard cormorant shrieks; and, far beyond,
Where the great ocean mingles with the sky,
Behold the cloud-like islands grey in mist.

Humphry Davy, lines contributed to *An English Anthology.*

St Michael's Mount

Ay me! whilst thee the shores and sounding seas
Wash far away, — where'er thy bones are hurl'd,
Whether beyond the stormy Hebrides
Where thou perhaps, under the whelming tide,
Visitest the bottom of the monstrous world;
Or whether thou, to our moist views denied,
Sleep'st by the fable of Bellerus old,
Where the great Vision of the guarded mount
Looks towards Namancos and Bayona's hold,
— Look homeward Angel, now, and melt with ruth:
— And, O ye dolphins, waft the hapless youth!

Milton, from *Lycidas.*

(The reference to the Angel is to an ancient tradition that the archangel Michael appeared to some hermits, supposedly upon a large rock overhanging the old battery, known as St Michael's Chair.)

10

Last of England

Every English county commands the deep loyalty of its partisans, and for none is this local patriotism more passionately felt than for Cornwall. The counties are themselves divided into a number of smaller areas or regions, each with its own highly distinctive character, and for them is reserved the warmer, more intimate affection given only to things which lie nearest the heart. It is with one of these sub-divisions that we are concerned here — the Penwith district of Cornwall, known to Diodorus Siculus and the ancient world as Belerium, but more familiar to later ages as Land's End, the tip of the long peninsula which thrusts westwards into the Atlantic Ocean to divide the English from St George's Channel. Last of England and of Cornwall; last to have cherished, also, the dying Celtic tongue of our ancestors and many fabulous legends from the olden times; but assuredly *first* in the magic of its irresistible appeal to resident and stranger alike. For this is a hauntingly beautiful land, pervaded by powerful influences from a mysterious past; small wonder that so many believe it to be a little piece of Paradise misplaced, and call it with true feeling 'God's own country'.

Penwith is one of the nine ancient Cornish 'hundreds'. This term dates back to Anglo-Saxon times, and probably originally signified either that a hundred free families lived in the district, or that it contained a hundred hides of land. The name 'Penwith' at first denoted only the point of Land's End itself, but was by degrees extended to the West Penwith peninsula — that near-island west of a line drawn from St Erth bridge to Marazion — and then to the entire hundred, which stretched eastwards to Illogan and Scorrier. On the reorganisation of local government in 1974, a new Penwith District Council was established, with territory reaching as far as Gwithian, Gwinear, St Hilary and Perranuthnoe, making it co-extensive with the ecclesiastical Deanery of Penwith. This is the area covered by the present book.

An early form of the name, dating back to 997 and mentioned by P. A. S. Pool in *The Place Names of West Penwith*, is 'Penwith steort', which corresponds closely to the modern name of Land's End in both Cornish (*Penwith*, extreme end) and Old English (*steort*, tail or end). So in whatever language, the name has remained unchanged for a thousand years at least, an indication of the long-continuing fascination of the place's unique geographical situation.

Despite its limited extent, Penwith embraces an astonishing range of topographical features, from wave-shattered metamorphic cliffs fissured by fearsome zawns (deep clefts) on the bleak northern coast to the bold granitic grandeur of Land's End, with silver and golden sandy beaches at Gwithian, Hayle, St Ives, Sennen, Porthcurno, Marazion; warm, sheltered, south-facing farms around Penzance and Gulval, where flowers and vegetables flourish right though the mild winters; a great sweep of undulating cairn-crowned hills running from Trencrom in the east through Trink, Rosewall, Trendrine, Zennor and Carn

11

Galver to Chapel Carn Brea in the west; desolate moors and downs; spreading acres of lush pasture land; and a few charming tree-filled valleys, of which Lamorna is undoubtedly queen.

Penwith is ancient in both geological and human terms. Particularly towards the west, the cromlechs, menhirs, fogous, barrows, stone circles, beehive huts and hill and cliff castles of long-vanished races of men are brooding reminders of dead cultures and religions disturbingly different from our own. Later came the patiently created Celtic small-field pattern, each tiny enclosure bounded by lichened dry-stone walls; snug little hamlets and farms; grey parish churches, whose pinnacled towers sometimes stand stark and solitary upon the skyline, but are more often the nuclei of compact villages or small towns.

The mines, now quiet, left crumbling engine houses perched precariously on steep cliffsides or standing like petrified sentinels on remote hills, guardians of a ravaged treasure. Around the coast, ancient fishing coves still retain their piers and slipways, but the living industry is now largely concentrated at the busy port of Newlyn. In the present century, Penwith has experienced in full measure the impact of that all-pervasive new industry, tourism. Its uniquely varied attractions have brought visitors flocking here in their thousands, with dramatic and not always welcome effects on the environment. The changes have entailed losses as well as gains to the area, and its character has been much modified. The giants, piskies, fairies, spriggans, buccas, knockers and mermaids of local folk-lore, always shy and elusive creatures, have retreated into total invisibility before the flood of cars and coaches, and are scarcely remembered now.

Fortunately, the camera arrived just in time to record some aspects of the old order before it finally passed away. Through its lens, we may still glimpse the brown-sailed luggers of Mount's Bay and St Ives returning from the fishing grounds laden with catches of mackerel, or herring; ponderous beam engines and primitive water stamps busily at work on long-forgotten mines; spectacular shipwrecks; public rejoicings at great national and local events; the picturesque charm of ancient fishing coves, villages and towns before the ruthless hand of the improver had been laid upon them, and above all, people — performing their various daily tasks or enjoying the simple pleasures of a less hurried world than ours. To study such photographs is to gain a new historical perspective of the Penwith district and a deeper understanding of the manner in which its essential qualities evolved. They arouse nostalgia for vanished scenes and ways of life which seem sweeter in retrospect than they were in reality, but enrich and widen our appreciation of the past with a vividness which the written word can never capture.

OPPOSITE: Scattered throughout West Cornwall are directing posts and milestones carved during the first half of the nineteenth century by two eccentric rival 'poets' — Billy Foss of Sancreed and Henry Quick of Zennor. ABOVE LEFT: Milestone near Gurnard's Head, possibly by Henry Quick: 'St Ives 6M Penzance 6M', (WT) and CENTRE: stone at Trewey, probably the work of Quick. (WT) RIGHT: Milestone opposite Land's End Airport, dated AD 1836 and probably cut by Billy Foss. (WT) BELOW LEFT: St Erth-St Hilary directing post, on the road from St Erth to Rospeath. (WT) CENTRE: Directing post at Chun, said to be by Quick, but from its style more probably the work of Foss. (WT) RIGHT: In 1819 the old post at Tregerest (North Road) was 'the laughing stock of every traveller'. Billy Foss corrected the offending inscription, and a friend praised his work in verse:

'Who saw the old directing post,
As finished by Trevollian first,
Unless his senses all were lost,
That did not into laughter burst.

Friend Foss resolved at his first view
This shameful sculpture to deface
And the directions form anew,
To save his parish from disgrace.

This work now done, to places nigh
The Post an ornament shall stand
And long shall shew the passing eye
The sculpture of an able hand.' (WT)

Directing post, Methodist chapel and Celtic cross at Crows-an-Wra, forming a typical West Cornish rural scene. The post is a good example of Billy Foss's highly ornamental style. (WT)

14

Madron & Penzance

The ancient parish of Madron, with Morvah, stretched from sea to sea across the Penwith peninsula and until 1871 included the former Borough of Penzance. Its name was originally spelt, and is still often pronounced 'Maddern', from St Madern (otherwise Padern, Patern or Baden), the patron saint.

Near the road from Madron to Morvah stands the most famous of Madron's many reminders of early man, the Lanyon cromlech. Its capstone, thrown down in a great storm in 1816, was replaced in 1824, using the same tackle with which Lieut. Goldsmith replaced the Logan Rock at Treen. West Lanyon cromlech is half a mile away, and there is also an imperfect cromlech on Mulfra Hill. At Bossulow Downs stands the curious monument called the Men-an-tol, or 'holed stone', set between two monoliths. It is also known as the 'crick stone', from the belief that it would afford relief to sufferers from backache who crawled through the hole in a certain way. Near it stands the famous Men-scryfa or 'stone of writing' bearing the inscription *Rialobrani Cunovalli Fili*: 'Rialobran, son of Cunovall'. At Penzance is the great Iron Age castle of Lescudjack, while west of the town is a small earthwork called Lesingey Round, with another at Mount Misery, north-west of Tolcarne.

During the 6th century, St Madern, thought to have been a bishop, came to Cornwall from Brittany and took up his abode in a marsh about a mile north of Madron churchtown. Here he built a baptistery, near what has become his holy well. The water rises from a hole two feet square and used to run in an open stream round the hill, through the village and down to Penzance, where it formed the main water supply, reaching the sea at Sandy Bank. The original building has disappeared; the existing 14th century one, measuring 24 ft by 10 ft, though roofless, is still occasionally used.

The water became famed for its healing properties; children were dipped, invalids washed, prayers offered and miracles allegedly wrought. The most remarkable of these occurred to John Trelille, who was baptised at Madron on 18 November 1610. Dr Hall, Bishop of Exeter, stated in his *Treatise on the Invisible World* (1652) that Trelille was so badly crippled by the contraction of his leg sinews that for sixteen years he walked upon his hands. Admonished in a dream, Trelille washed himself in Madron Well and was so restored that Dr Hall saw him able to walk and get his living. He eventually joined the King's army, 'where he behaved himself with great stoutness both of mind and body', and was killed at Lyme in 1644.

Much of the original undivided parish of Madron belonged to the Domesday manor of Alverton (Alwarton), named after its pre-Conquest Saxon owner Alward, and centred on Alverton Farm, Penzance. It was given by William I to his half-brother Robert, Count of Mortain. Trengwainton and Landithy, together with the advowson of the church, formed an outlying part of the manor of Roseworthy (Ritwore) in Gwinear. Roseworthy was granted in the 12th century to the de la Pomerai family, one of whom, around 1150, gave the church of 'St Madernus de Rydwori' to the Knights Hospitallers. Henry de la Pomerai suffered confiscation of his lands for leading Prince John's rebellion of 1197 against Richard I in Cornwall, and in 1203 King John granted the church to Thomas de Chimelly for life, but following an objection, the Knights of St John recovered their rights.

Gyrardus de Curmerniaco was Rector of the Church of St Madernus in 1276, but in 1278 a vicar was instituted on the presentation of the Prior of the Hospital of St John in England, so between these years the benefice was finally appropriated to the priory, which enjoyed the great tithes until the Dissolution in 1538. Landithy estate, adjoining the church, was given to the priory with the advowson; it may have comprised the demesnes of a Celtic monastery. The remains of a grange or country house probably belonging to the Hospital are said to have survived here until the last century.

A font has survived from the Norman church of Madron, which stood on the site of the present south aisle. In 1936 an even earlier inscribed stone, of the 8th century, was found built into the south-west wall. It has been variously read as 'QONRA FILIA TAENNAE', commemorating a hypothetical Cornish princess, and 'AIA HELNOTH'. The present chancel and south arcade were built before 1336, when the altar was consecrated by Bishop Grandisson on 13 July. A panel of ten coloured and gilded alabaster angels, probably part of a 14th century shrine or reredos, is the special treasure of the church, which has a 14th century tower.

The church contains memorials to John Clies (1568-1623), who became the second Mayor of Penzance in October 1614, and John Maddern (d. 1621) whose father, 'John Maddern Gentleman', was the first Mayor in May 1614. There are also funeral hatchments of such well known families as Borlase, Price, Le Grice, Scoble, Armstrong, Tremenheere, Nicholls, Usticke, Robyns, Pascoe and Daniel. Alexander Daniel (d. 1668) and his son George (d. 1716), who founded the adjacent Church School, are buried in the churchyard.

The Nelson Banner is still borne in procession at the annual Trafalgar Service. News of Nelson's victory at Trafalgar was first brought to England on 4 November 1805 by a Penzance fishing boat, which intercepted HMS *Pickle*, under Lieut. Lapenotiere, returning from the battle. A ball in progress at the Assembly Rooms in Chapel Street (the present Union Hotel) was interrupted by the Mayor's announcement from the gallery, and it was decided to hold a memorial service for the fallen hero. The banner was hastily contrived for the occasion and carried in procession before the Mayor to Madron.

Penzance (*Pen sans*) may be translated as either 'holy head' or 'holy headland'; it was the former and obviously less appropriate interpretation which inspired the town's grisly insignia of John the Baptist's head on a charger. On 12 August 1429, Bishop Lacy licensed a Chapel of St Gabriel and St Raphael of Pensans, which is believed to have been situated at the south-west corner of Barbican Lane; around the year 1800 it was converted to a fish cellar. This may well have been the original chapel which gave the 'holy headland' its name. In 1850 a mutilated Gothic cross with figures was removed from the ruins of the building to St Mary's churchyard, by a mason who referred to it as 'St Raffidy', doubtless a corruption of 'Raphael'. Lake's *Parochial History* refers to the remains of a Chapel of St Anthony at the end of Barbican Lane, almost certainly the same building.

A little further inland stood St Mary's Chapel, on the site of the present parish church of St Mary the Virgin. This was already in existence in 1321, when 'an extent of the Manor of Alwertone' included a chapel in which mass was celebrated three days a week every year by the Prior of St Michael's Mount, if the lord was present. Sir Henry de Tyes, lord of Alverton, founded a chantry in the chapel and endowed it with £4 a year out of the lands of

16

the manor, but this endowment was lost at the Reformation. In 1662 St Mary's was rebuilt; old prints depict it as a quaint structure with a somewhat peculiar spire. By 1832 this building was inadequate for the needs of the growing population and was taken down, to be replaced in 1835 by the present church, the architect being Charles Hutchens of St Buryan. Its tall, lean tower dominates most parts of Penzance. A chapel of St Clare near the cemetery on the road to Madron gave its name to St Clare Street — 'Synt Clears Lane' in 1600. The notebook of Alexander Daniel, lord of Alverton, mentions in 1614 'Chapel Green' and 'the chapel iuxta Adjaporth', which the Corporation rented from him.

John Wesley visited Penzance on several occasions, at first encountering some hostility, but on 17 September 1760 he noted in his *Journal*: 'At noon I preached on the Cliff at Penzance where no one now gives us an uncivil word'. At noon on 13 April 1744 he preached on the Downs at Heamoor, standing on a convenient rock near the house of William John, a Penzance merchant, where he had been allowed to dry his rain-soaked clothes. This rock was afterwards used as a pulpit base in a chapel built at Heamoor, and was moved again into the new Wesley Rock Chapel which succeeded it. Other religious denominations represented at Penzance have included Congregationalists, Baptists, Quakers, Roman Catholics, Jews, the Plymouth Brethren and the Salvation Army.

In 1848 part of Madron parish was transferred to the new parish of St Peter's, Newlyn, where a church was completed in 1866. St Paul's Church, Penzance, built in 1842, became a parish church in 1867, and St Mary's in 1871; in 1973 the two were combined as a united benefice. In 1883 the parish of St John's, Penzance, was separated from St Mary's to serve the eastern part of the town. The Mission Church of St Thomas, Heamoor, was dedicated in 1892.

One of the many significant events in the story of Penzance occurred on 25 April 1332, when Alice de Lisle, sister of Lord Tyes, was granted a Wednesday market, with a seven day fair starting on 1 August at Penzance and another of the same duration at Mousehole on 24 August. Henry VIII, by a charter of 16 March 1512, granted the inhabitants of Penzance harbour and other dues, on condition that they kept the quay and bulwarks in repair. James I conferred borough status on Penzance by a Charter of Incorporation dated 9 May 1614, giving it a Mayor, eight Aldermen and twelve Councillors.

During the Civil War, in 1648, a Royalist rising at Penzance was suppressed by Parliamentary forces commanded by the Sheriff, Edward Herle, and Col. Robert Bennett, the town being plundered by the victorious soldiers. In 1663 Penzance was constituted a Coinage Town for the assessment and taxation of tin, an indication of the growing importance of this industry in West Cornwall. Much alarm was occasioned in 1760 when an Algerine corsair ran ashore near Newlyn with pirates on board, but the affair ended peacefully, the unwelcome visitors being returned to their own country by a ship of war. 1766 saw the building of the Old Pier, the structure being extended in 1785, 1812 and 1853; the Albert or North Pier was completed in 1847.

Penzance's greatest son, Sir Humphry Davy, was born on 17 December 1778 at 4 The Terrace, his parents' home. A man of many talents, he chose to devote himself to science; besides inventing the Davy lamp, which has saved the lives of thousands of coal miners, he discovered laughing gas, pioneered agricultural and electro-chemistry, demonstrated the true nature of chlorine, isolated the metals sodium and potassium by electrolytic methods and also made the first electric light — the arc lamp. His early friendship with Southey and Coleridge reveals another side to his character, and Coleridge said of him that had he not devoted himself to science, he would have shone with the highest lustre as a poet. The delightful anecdotes of his youthful escapades at Penzance have won him a sure place in the memory of his townsfolk.

In the early 19th century, the exceptionally mild winters enjoyed by this district attracted an increasing number of invalids to Penzance. The publication in 1816 of Dr J. A. Paris's *Guide to the Mount's Bay*, one of the first Cornish guide books, marked the beginning of a migration to the south-west which has since grown into the fantastic annual tourist invasion of modern times. Two cultural institutions which still flourish were established in 1814 and 1818 respectively: the Royal Geological Society of Cornwall and the Penzance Library. The old Market House was taken down in 1836, while 1843 witnessed the construction of the Western Promenade. The West Cornwall Railway opened between Penzance and Truro on 25 August 1852, direct communication with Paddington being established in 1859, on the completion of the Royal Albert Bridge at Saltash. The Public Buildings (including St John's Hall) were opened in September 1867 to great public rejoicing, and the School of Art followed in 1880, while 1884 saw the opening of the Floating Dock.

Penzance has the distinction of having been the first Cornish port to possess a lifeboat; one was provided in 1803 by local subscription, together with a donation of £50 from Lloyds. She was never launched on service and was sold to cover rent debts in 1812, but in later years, Penzance lifeboats performed many gallant rescues. The station was closed in 1917, but another, opened at Newlyn in 1908, was replaced in 1913 by the present Penlee, where the boat is launched from her house by a direct slipway.

The borough boundaries were enlarged in 1934 to include parts of Gulval and Madron parishes and nearly the whole of Paul. However, in the comprehensive reorganisation of local government of 1974, Penzance forfeited its ancient borough status altogether, being united with the former Borough of St Ives, St Just Urban District and West Penwith Rural District to form a new Penwith District Council, with offices at St Clare. A Charter Trust has been established to safeguard the old borough regalia, with a Town Mayor to maintain the dignity and honour of that ancient office and serve as a focus of civic pride.

The grant by the King of Arms by Warrant of the Earl Marshal of a Coat of Arms to the Borough of Penzance, dated 12 June 1934. (PCT, WT)

ABOVE: Madron parish church *c*1860. (DT, MD) BELOW: The interior of the church prior to its restoration, *c*1880. The window was removed to Heamoor, where it is now the west window of St Thomas' Church. (WR)

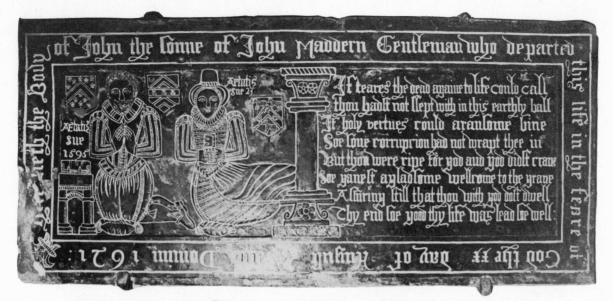

ABOVE: Slate memorial in Madron church to John Maddern, son of 'John Maddern gentleman', first Mayor of Penzance. (WR, WT) CENTRE: The burial of Alexander Daniel recorded in Madron parish register. (WR, WT) BELOW LEFT: Madron handbell ringers at their final concert on 5 July 1977. On the right is the vicar, the Rev William Rowett. (WR, TF) RIGHT: The bell of the Ding Dong mine at Madron church. Last rung in 1878 to bring up the final shift of miners, it was presented to Madron Old Cornwall Society in 1961. (WR, WT)

ABOVE: Canon H. R. Jennings (wearing mortar board) on the Diocesan
Pilgrimage to Madron Baptistery, August 1927. The service was attended
by the Bishop of Truro, the Rt Rev Dr Frere, and many Cornish clergy.
(WR) BELOW: Wesley Rock Chapel, Heamoor, drawn and engraved by
William Willis.

21

LEFT: Men Scryfa, Madron. (CCL) ABOVE: King William the Fourth public house, Madron. (AE) BELOW: An excursion party leaves Heamoor for the Logan Rock, c1905. (DT)

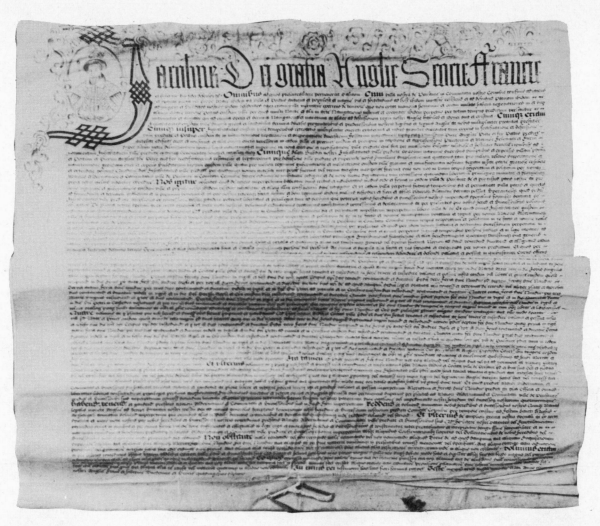

ABOVE: The Charter of Incorporation granted by James I to the Borough of Penzance, 9 May 1614. (PHM, WT) BELOW: Part of the Penzance regalia. (PCT, WT)

ABOVE LEFT: The upper end of Market Jew Street, a drawing from Dr Paris' *Guide to the Mount's Bay* (1824 ed). It shows Sir Humphry Davy's first laboratory, the first house on the left of the ascending footway, beneath the clock of the Market House tower. INSET: Sir Humphry Davy, and RIGHT: laying the wreath at his centenary commemoration, 8 June 1929 (for 29 May 1829). Sir Ambrose Fleming, inventor of the thermionic valve, represented the Royal Institution and is in the centre with his hand raised. (PHM) BELOW LEFT: The Wherry Mine, Penzance, (PHM) and RIGHT: the engine house on shore. (CCL) The mine began operation *c*1700. Abandoned soon afterwards, it was reopened in 1798 by Thomas Curtis of Breage and later acquired by a company including Richard Pearce, Mayor of Penzance. It closed in 1838 after the staging was knocked down by an American barque on Gwavas Lake during a gale.

24

ABOVE LEFT: Old Penzance Market House, demolished in 1836. (PHM)
RIGHT: The badge of the Penzance Borough Police Force, amalgamated
with the county force on 1 April 1947. It incorporates the old borough seal,
showing John the Baptist's head on a charger. (PHM, WT) BELOW: Old
St Mary's Chapel, Penzance, drawn in 1832 shortly before its demolition.

ABOVE: Penzance from Castle Horneck, 1834-5. (PHM) BELOW: The upper end of Market Jew Street. The two fishwives are wearing 'cowels' or baskets on their backs, supported by a band around the forehead. The porch of the Star Inn was demolished in 1860.

27

ABOVE: Penzance fire engine in 1907. This is believed to have been the machine purchased in 1742-3 together with twelve leather buckets, for a total of £10 11s 6d. (PHM) BELOW: The borough police force in front of St John's Hall. (R)

ABOVE: Laying the foundation stone of the North Pier, 7 July 1845. Following the Prince Consort's landing there in September 1846, its name was changed to the Albert Pier. (PHM) BELOW: The original Penzance railway station, opened in 1852. The present station dates from 1879.

Quay Street *c*1900, looking towards St Mary's Church. (PHM)

ABOVE: Causewayhead entrance from Greenmarket. (PHM) BELOW:
Coinagehall Street, with steps to Quay Street. (PHM)

ABOVE: The *Leon Bureau* at Penzance. The Ross swing bridge was opened in 1881. (PHM) BELOW: The *Victoria* horse 'bus arriving at Penzance from Land's End. (G)

LEFT: 'Old Davey', a watercress seller at Penzance c1900. (PHM) ABOVE:
The inscribed 11th century Penzance Market Cross in the wall of the
Market House. It is now at Penlee. (PHM) BELOW: Water wheel at
Rosehill, Penzance. (PHM, R)

ABOVE: An Edwardian summertime scene on Penzance Promenade,
(CRO) and BELOW: storm damage to the promenade. (R)

34

Paul

The parish of Paul makes a special claim on the hearts of all Cornish people as the last place where the ancient language of the Duchy was spoken, before its final extinction in the late 18th century. Its name is derived from St Paul, or Paulinus, who founded the diocese of Leon in Brittany, and who may possibly have built the first church in this part of Cornwall. Paul lay entirely within the extensive royal manor of Alverton, which belonged in the mid-13th century to Earl Richard, King of the Romans. In 1246 he was nearly drowned in a terrible storm when returning to Cornwall from Gascony, and having vowed to build a Cistercian monastery if he escaped, Richard founded the Abbey of Hailes in Gloucestershire, which was completed in 1251. As part of its endowment, he gave the new abbey the church of Paul in 1259.

On 11 July of that year, Roger de Sancto Constantino, one of the King's Clerks and a man of some distinction, was instituted Rector of St Paulinus. In 1266 he obtained a licence for a yearly fair on the Vigil, Feast and Morrow of St Paulinus, and a year later was granted a charter for a Thursday market in his manor of Portheness (Mousehole), together with an annual fair on the Vigil, Feast and Morrow of St Matthias. Roger was the last rector at Paul, the Abbot and Convent at Hailes, who were themselves rectors, thereafter appointing vicars to the parish. The earliest known was John, a turbulent character frequently at odds with the authorities. On 26 October 1308, the king issued a writ to the bishop, stating that Ralph de Kerres (Kerris, in Paul) had summoned John, Vicar of the Church of St Paul of Bruony (sometimes spelt Brewinney, the old Celtic name of the lands adjoining Paul village) to answer for an alleged assault on the plaintiff at Mousehole, in which he had beaten and wounded him and removed certain muniments. The bishop ordered a sequestration of one mark.

The church was rebuilt or heavily repaired in the early 14th century, and in 1315 Bishop Stapledon was requested to consecrate four new altars, but failed to do so. However, the high altar was dedicated on 11 July 1336.

The name of Mousehole is locally said to have originated from the cavern in the cliff just beyond the village, and this may well be correct, since the earliest forms of the name — Mushal (1284), Mosehole (1300), etc. — differ little from the modern English spelling. However, Richard Edmonds suggested in 1862 that it came from '*moz-hel*' or '*mouz-hel*', 'the maid's brook or river', an allusion to the stream running through the village close to the doors of the women who used it; and indeed, 'Mouzel' is still the accepted pronunciation. The most interesting of Paul's numerous chapels stood on the little St Clement's Isle a quarter of a mile off Mousehole quay, which may have given the village its old Cornish name of Porthenys — island beach or cove. Leland described it in 1540 as 'a lytle low island with a chaple yn yt. And this lytle islet bereth gresse', but no trace of the chapel now remains. St Clement was the patron saint of ships, and it is possible that the chapel, in such an extraordinary place, was intended to display a guiding light for shipping.

A chapel of the Blessed Virgin Mary at Mousehole was licensed on 2 September 1383, but by 1414 it had been 'ruinated by the sea'. Insufficient money being available for its repair, Bishop Stafford offered an indulgence of forty days to all who contributed, since 'it had long been a useful landmark (to the saving of many lives) for vessels entering the narrow harbour'. It was relicensed on 15 January 1420 as St Mary and St Eda. In 1440 a chapel was being built in Mousehole, dedicated to St Edmund of Canterbury, otherwise St Edmund the Confessor.

In 1300 Edward I had granted Baron Henry de Tyes a Tuesday market and a three day fair at Mousehole on the Eve, Day and Morrow of St Barnabas the Apostle, with free warren (rights to game) over his royal manor of Alverton.

Mousehole was then the largest population centre in Mount's Bay, and a port much frequented by traders with Spain. This connection was illustrated in 1301, when William Cosyn and others broke by night into a house at Mousehole in which were wax and other goods and chattels of some Spanish merchants, which they took to the value of £5. John le Cotithen received the stolen goods and carried them off to Devonshire. In 1356 the Penwith jury protested that a certain Ralph Vyvyan had extorted money from five people at Newlyn and Mousehole, taken two oxen, worth twenty shillings, from Vincent Morveck 'quite contrary to the will of Vincent', and that 'he and his son took John Dinion and other Spanish merchants prisoners at Mousehole and kept them until they paid 100s. Whereupon they fled the country with their merchandise to the great hurt of the traders and merchants.' It was not always the visitors who suffered, for when 'Adam of Donewyth, Roger le Lung, called the Granger, Robert Peytenen de la Moghel, David, son of Alan of Cork and certain other worthy mariners came to Mousehole in a ship of Cork' and sought to obtain provisions from Mark, a merchant, and Reginald de Gascoyn 'at their own will' and were refused, they returned to their ship, took up arms and went into the town, where they searched out Mark and slew Dennis 'his man', robbed Mark of 58s and fled.

In 1435 Bishop Lacy granted an indulgence to those contributing to the building and repair of Mousehole quay. In the days of sailing ships, Mousehole was the principal centre for pilotage in Mount's Bay; some pilot boats operated in the Bay itself, while others took vessels up the Bristol Channel and on to Liverpool, or through the English Channel to Dover. Both pilchard and mackerel seines were kept here, together with mackerel-drivers, pilchard-drivers, jolly boats, yawls and crabbers, built in the open air on the bank near the Old Pier, from oak cut in Lamorna and Trewoofe valleys. The quay was extended in 1840 and a new pier added about twenty years later. Many hundreds were then employed in fishing and its ancillary industries, but a great decline set in, and the village now gets its living from tourism.

In 1437 a further indulgence was granted by the Bishop of Exeter to those contributing to the building of Newlyn's quay, the little curved structure still to be seen within the present harbour. The name Newlyn is derived from the Old English for 'new pool'. For centuries Newlyn remained inferior in size and importance to Mousehole; but during the 18th century its fisheries greatly increased, and by the mid-19th century it employed the greatest number of drift boats in Cornwall. It was also a centre of the seine fishery, and pilchards caught near the Lizard were brought to Newlyn by sea for curing. The small harbour was by this time quite inadequate, and the fishermen's difficulties were aggravated by the arrival of a large fleet of east coast boats for the spring mackerel fishery. A magnificent new harbour was built, the South Pier being completed in 1885, and the North Pier in 1888. In May 1896 Newlyn was the scene of two days' riot, when a long-standing dispute between the Sabbatarian Cornish fishermen and the 'Yorkies', over the vexed Sunday fishing issue, broke into open hostilities. Military and naval forces had to be called in to quell the trouble. Newlyn is today one of the principal fishing ports in the south-west, quite a different place from the 'lesser fishing town' reduced to ashes by marauding Spaniards four hundred years ago.

The story of the burning of Mousehole, Newlyn and Penzance by the Spaniards is well known. According to Richard Carew, four galleys appeared off Mousehole just after dawn on 23 July 1595 and landed 200 pike and shot who burned both the village and Paul church, the inhabitants fleeing in terror. Re-embarking their men, the galleys moved on to Newlyn, where they put ashore 400 men, who marched up the hill and saw in the distance a small force which Sir Francis Godolphin had hastily assembled at Penzance to resist them. The Spaniards marched towards Penzance while the galleys fired on the defenders, causing them to disperse and run away. Sir Francis endeavoured to rally his men in the Market Place, but only two resolute shot and his own servants, about fourteen all told, remained by him. Meeting with practically no resistance, the enemy set fire to Penzance and Newlyn and returned to their ships. Next day they again tried to land on the eastern side of the bay, but made off on seeing the better organised Cornish forces now ranged against them.

Another version of the burning of Mousehole was published by a local resident, who signed himself 'Nota Bene, alias Mem. F.A.S.', in the *Royal Cornwall Gazette* of 16 May 1807. He described how, when some slates were removed from the roof of the south porch of Paul church for repairs, marks of the fire which had partially injured it were found on a wooden supporter. Bodinnar, the carpenter, realised the significance of his discovery and preserved the burnt wood, which was distributed among the neighbouring gentlemen. 'It is curious to observe how the circumstance of a *single* supporter of the roof of the porch being burnt, and that the one nearest the body of the church, confirms part of the tradition, which prevails in our parish: viz. that the Spaniards met some women carrying wood and furze, which they compelled the women to carry into the church, and put it near the *south* porch, the door of which they set open to receive the blast of strong *south* wind, which prevailed that day. The direction of the wind consumed the church, but preserved the porch . . . The thick stone division at the back of Trewarveneth seat, which has puzzled many people, is a part of the old church, which escaped the fire. — There is a tradition that a farmer's wife found a Spaniard drunk and asleep in a corn field, and that she cut his throat with a sickle; and another tradition is, that a farmer cunningly set his furze rick on fire, and ran from it in apparent trepidation, by which the Spaniards were deceived, and, thinking that one of their parties had fired the village, passed by without molesting it.'

Paul parish registers were destroyed in the raid; Vicar John Tremearne began the new burial register with a short memorandum on the burning of the church, together with the names of three local people who died in the raid: 'Jenken Keigwin of Mowsholl being kild by the Spaniards was Buried the 24th of Julij. Jacobius de Newlen occisus fuit per inimicos et sepultes est 26 die Julij. Similites Teek Cornall et sepultus the 26th of Julij.'

Jenken Keigwin, then principal inhabitant of Mousehole, was killed by a cannon ball which was still preserved when Davies Gilbert wrote (*c*1830) 'and to within these few years an implacable hatred was entertained against the very name of a Spaniard'. The Keigwin family lived in the old house known as the Keigwin Arms. John Keigwin, born in 1641, was a noted authority on the Cornish language, and his translations into English of *Mount*

37

Calvary and *The Creation of the World with Noah's Flood* were printed by Davies Gilbert, with the original Cornish texts. He died about 1710, and family disputes led to the dispersal of his estates. The manor house was bought by an old family servant named John Wills, out of respect for his former employers, and he kept it for many years as an inn. He also acquired the Keigwin pews, which occupied a large part of the church, permitting no one, not even himself, to enter them. When he was eventually forced to give them up, as the *Sherborne Mercury* reported, 'the grief occasioned by the removal of the bones of his ancient benefactor, to prepare a space for the erection of new pews and a vault for their present possessor', hastened his death in 1800 at the age of 89.

Mousehole's most celebrated character was Dorothy (Dolly) Pentreath, popularly considered the last traditional speaker of the Cornish tongue. Dolly herself claimed that she knew no word of English until past twenty years of age. Her father was a fisherman, and as a child of twelve she sold fish at Penzance in Cornish, which the ordinary inhabitants, and even the gentry, well understood. Daines Barrington interviewed her in 1768, when she was an old woman, and published virtually all the information we have regarding her. Dolly died nine years later, her burial (under her married name of Jeffery) being recorded in Paul register on 27 December. In 1860 Prince Louis Lucien Bonaparte, a keen student of old languages, set up a memorial stone to her in the churchyard wall facing the road, which incorrectly gives the year of her death as 1778. Within the church is another monument to a worthy upholder of the language in its latter days, Capt. Stephen Hutchens, RN (d. 1709). It contains the only inscription in Cornish dating from a time when it was still in daily use. The little couplet may be freely rendered as

> 'Eternal bliss be his whose loving care
> Gave Paul an almshouse and the church repair.'

ABOVE: A Mousehole charter of 1300 (see Appendix I). (PRO) BELOW LEFT: The memorial to three young fishermen missionaries outside Paul church. (RHC, WT) RIGHT: Captain Stephen Hutchens' memorial in the church: 'Life without end is the reward of your kindness to the poor folk of Paul and our church'. (RHC, WT)

The entry in the parish register recording the burial of those killed in the Spanish raid of 1595. (RHC, WT) INSET: Paul parish church. (RHC, WT)

ABOVE LEFT: Dolly Pentreath's cottage at
CENTRE: Her memorial in Paul churchyard, (RHC
Prince Louis Lucien Bonaparte, who erected the m
The Keigwin Arms, Mousehole. (M) ABOVE RIGH
whose bi-centenary was celebrated at Paul chu
Christmas Gwesperow (Evensong) in Cornish, (M
burial of Dorothy Jeffery (Pentreath) recorded in
(RHC, WT)

40

HERE LIETH INTERRED
DOROTHY PENTREATH
WHO DIED IN
1777
SAID TO HAVE BEEN THE
LAST PERSON WHO CONVERSED
IN THE ANCIENT CORNISH
THE PECULIAR LANGUAGE OF
THIS COUNTY FROM THE
EARLIEST RECORDS
TILL IT EXPIRED IN THE
EIGHTEENTH CENTURY
IN THIS PARISH OF
SAINT PAUL.

THIS STONE IS ERECTED BY
THE PRINCE
LOUIS LUCIEN BONAPARTE
IN UNION WITH
THE REVᴰ JOHN GARRETT
VICAR OF ST PAUL
JUNE 1860

HONOUR THY FATHER AND THY MOTHER
THAT THY DAYS MAY BE LONG UPON
THE LAND WHICH THE LORD THY GOD
GIVETH THEE   EXOD. XX 12
GWRA PERTHI DE TAZ HA DE MAM
MAL DE DYTHIOW BETHENZ HYR WAR
AN TYR NEO AN ARLETH DE DEW
RYES DEES   EXOD. XX 12

e. (M, G)
BELOW:
M) LEFT:
Pentreath,
77 with a
LOW: the
sh register.

Burials in the Year 1777. Continued.

Dorothy Jeffery was buried December 27.

*This is the famous dolly Pentreath the maiden
spoken of by Daines Barrington in the Archæolog*

Burials in the Year 1778.

41

ABOVE: Mousehole and Mount's Bay, and BELOW: Mousehole in 1891.
(PHM)

ABOVE: Mousehole and St Clement's Island. (CRO, FF) BELOW:
Mousehole harbour, 1891. (PHM, FF)

43

ABOVE: A view of Mousehole, (CT) and LEFT: Duck Street in 1931.
(PHM) RIGHT: The 1,100 ton freeze trawler *Conqueror* on the rocks near
Mousehole on 27 December 1977. She had just caught 250 tonnes of
mackerel off Penzer Point. The £1 million trawler, on her first voyage after
a major refit at Hull, was declared a total loss. (WT)

ABOVE: Newlyn from Tolcarn, by J. T. Blight, *c*1850. BELOW: Gwavas
Quay, Newlyn, in 1831, by J. S. Prout. (CCL)

ABOVE: Newlyn, (CRO) and BELOW: its harbour. (CRO, FF)

46

ABOVE: Newlyn; a sign on one of the buildings reads 'Paul Sail Maker'.
(CCL) BELOW: Fish quay, Newlyn. (DT)

47

ABOVE: New Harbour Road, Newlyn, (DT) and BELOW: the narrow gauge locomotive *Penlee,* which hauled roadstone from Penlee Quarry to Newlyn harbour for shipment. (R)

ABOVE: Newlyn fish market. (CRO) BELOW: Newlyn Court, 1906. (PHM)

ABOVE: Boleigh Farm, where Athelstan defeated the Cornish and their
Danish allies in AD 931. (AE) BELOW: The first Cornish Gorsedd at
Boscawen-un stone circle, 1928. (R)

St Buryan

The tall tower of St Buryan church forms a distinctive landmark visible over much of the Penwith peninsula. The church is dedicated to St Berriona, an Irish virgin who, according to the 11th century *Exeter Martyrology*, cured the son of King Gerentius (Geraint) of paralysis. She was commemorated both in the Diocese and in Ireland on 1 May; in the parish, her feast is still kept on the Sunday nearest to old May Day (13 May). Her *Life*, kept in the church, was probably destroyed at the Reformation; but John Leland, who seems to have read it in 1535, quotes from it to the effect that 'St Buriena a holy woman of Ireland sumtyme dwellid in this place and there made an oratory'.

The Dons Meyn (Dancing Stones) or Merry Maidens stand near the road on Roslucombe Farm (not Rosmodres, as is often stated), reminders of St Buryan's distant past. These standing stones are supposedly girls turned to stone for dancing on a Sunday, together with the 'Two Pipers' nearby, who provided them with music. Another circle on Boscawen-un Farm goes by the name of the Nine Maidens — they actually number nineteen, with a single menhir in the centre. The first meeting of the Cornish Gorsedd took place here in 1928.

Around the year 931, King Athelstan, pursuing the policy of his predecessors (Egbert and Alfred) in saxonising Cornwall, provoked a rebellion of the Cornish and their Danish allies, led by one Havel. He suppressed it in a great battle lasting several days, fought at Boleigh Farm, near Lamorna, in St Buryan. According to tradition, the dead were buried in a vault beneath the farmyard, and there are the remains of several barrows in the vicinity. The menhirs known as the Pipers are traditionally the Peace Stones set up between the opposing armies.

After spending the night at the 6th century St Buryan's oratory, Athelstan sailed with his victorious army to the Scilly Islands, to drive the Danes from their last stronghold on English soil. Before leaving, he vowed that if the expedition was successful he would build and endow a church on the site of the oratory, and returning triumphant, he drew up a charter to this effect, dated at Kingston, 6 October 943. By this, the king made a tax-free grant of land to the clergy who, living together under Celtic monastic rule, then staffed the Oratory of St Buryan, requiring as quit-rent 100 Masses, 100 Psalters and daily prayers. The cost of building the promised church, according to the Rev C. B. Crofts, would have been defrayed by fines extracted from the defeated inhabitants of Scilly. The original charter no longer exists, having been lost in a fire, but a copy has been preserved, made on the order of Bishop Brewer when he visited St Buryan to consecrate an enlarged church on 26 August 1238. Many of the place names mentioned in this manuscript remain in use, their spelling in some cases unchanged.

King Athelstan granted St Buryan church the valuable privilege of a Chartered or Extended Sanctuary. This meant that a robber taking refuge there had not only the usual right to obtain his freedom by returning the plunder and paying a fine, and a murderer that of either going into exile or standing trial in a civil court, but they could, after taking certain oaths to keep the peace, live permanently within the area of the sanctuary and there pursue their normal craft or business. In 1278 the Sanctuary was violated when Ivo the Weaver, then residing there, was arrested by the Sheriff. Leland said in 1533 that St Buryan had 'a Sanctuary whereby nere to the Church, be not above viii dwelling howses'. It remained in existence until about 1560. An early tombstone still survives, with a Norman-French inscription which reads: 'Clarice the wife of Geoffrey de Bolleit lies here, God of her soul have mercy, who pray for her soul shall have ten days pardon'.

The College of Secular Canons established by Athelstan consisted of a dean and three prebendaries. Until 1300 the visitorial rights of the bishops were maintained without objection, and the deans were installed by them on the presentation of the Earls of Cornwall. The dean was also lord of the manor of St Berian, called Eglosberria in the Exeter Domesday. In 1302 Ralph de Manton was granted a weekly Saturday market here, and two yearly three-day fairs on the Feasts of St Burian and St Martin.

Following Earl Edmund's death, the Earldom reverted to Edward I. In 1318 Edward II appointed as Dean of Buryan John de Maunte, the Queen's Clerk, a thoroughly unprincipled Frenchman, and prohibited the bishop from exercising any jurisdiction in the chapel, claiming that it was a Royal Free Chapel outside episcopal control. This was actually a fabrication by de Maunte, a pluralist, who wished it to be proved a sinecure. So began a long and bitter law suit between the Crown and the Bishop of Exeter, the verdict being given quite unjustly for the Crown. The court ruled that the parish was a Royal Peculiar, Sinecure and Donative, and that the bishop and archdeacon had no jurisdiction.

The dispute was marked by some lively proceedings. Dean John and his prebendary, Richard de Beaupré, who had been appointed by the bishop, soon quarrelled, and in 1327 a free-for-all brawl in the churchyard ended in bloodshed. The prebend broke the church door to take away his tithe, and the Sheriff arrested both him and the dean, with nearly all the leading parishioners of St Buryan — Boscawens, Vyvyans, Penroses, Brays, Penders and others — 43 in all. As a result, on 4 November 1328, at St Michael's Mount, Bishop Walter pronounced the Greater Excommunication against all who had laid violent hands on Richard de Beaupré and his supporters, and also interdicted the churchyard desecrated by the shedding of blood. In reply, the King served writs on both the bishop and Beaupré; but when in 1329 he ordered the bishop to collect the Tenth which had been granted him by the clergy, the bishop stated that he was 'afraid to meddle with St Buryan, for no one belonging to him dares to go there for fear of death and mutilation'.

The parish remained in this unfortunate state until 12 July 1336, when the bishop visited St Buryan in the course of a progress through Cornwall. The parishioners promised to submit to his authority, and he absolved them from the sentence of excommunication. He delivered an appropriate sermon in Latin (I Peter II, 25) which the Vicar of St Just translated into Cornish and others into English and French. But this was a short-lived triumph, being virtually the last effective intervention by the bishop in the affairs of the deanery.

Since Athelstan's visit in 931, the advowson had been held by the Crown, but in 1336 it passed to the Duchy of Cornwall. The character of the deans appointed, and the lack of ecclesiastical authority, had deplorable consequences on the spiritual welfare of the parishioners. Writing in 1351 to the Bishop of Worcester, Bishop Grandisson of Exeter said of the St Buryan people: 'Who below the Apostolic See can absolve them for their enormous crimes and excesses? I am silent concerning mere rumour, but it is lawful to speak of what is manifest to all. Since these men are in the tail of the world, they are constituted almost like wild beasts, they contract marriages in every prohibited degree and are divorced in every lawful one'. The scandal grew to such proportions that in 1473 a commission of clergymen was set up to prepare a scheme of reform, but they recommended only the pulling down of the old church and the building of the present one, leaving the abuses uncorrected.

The neglect of St Buryan by a succession of venal, drunken, incompetent, non-resident office holders continued until 1817, when the Hon Fitzroy Henry Richard Stanhope, a Peninsular War veteran who had lost a leg at Waterloo, was appointed the last dean by the Prince of Wales, on the recommendation of his brother, the Duke of York. So unfitted was this ignorant and illiterate man for the position, that no English bishop could be found to ordain him. However, when the Duke of York's sycophantic friend, the Bishop of Cork, was on holiday in London, Stanhope brought him a letter from the Prince, which read: 'Dear Cork, Please ordain Stanhope. Yours York'. Stanhope came back bearing the following reply: 'Dear York, Stanhope is now ordained. Yours Cork'. During the next 47 years, he collected tithes amounting to £60,000 from the parish, without once setting foot in St Buryan, except for a visit to 'read himself in'. On his death in 1864 an Act of Parliament returned the parish to the bishop, the deanery being abolished and St Sennen and St Levan constituted separate rectories. So ended the scandal of five centuries.

With its southerly aspect and rich granitic soil, St Buryan today boasts a number of excellent farms. The Vyvyans of Trelowarren originated from Trevedren and the Boscawens (Lord Falmouth's family) from Boscawenros, while William Noye (1577-1643), Attorney General under Charles I and principal contriver of the notorious ship-money tax, was born at Pendrea. Along the coast of the parish are several small fishing coves, among them Lamorna, with its lovely wooded valley, from which granite from a cliffside quarry was shipped during the last century. This valley leads up to Trewoofe (pronounced Trove) an ancient manor house which figures extensively in local folk-lore. St Loy's Cove took its name from a small chapel built on the verge of the cliff, whose remains, according to Blight in 1861, were toppled into the sea to gain a few extra feet of land for early crops. The stream that flows down the valley to Penberth Cove divides St Buryan parish from St Levan, to the west.

Athelstan's charter to St Buryan. (DRO, Diocese of Exeter)

ABOVE LEFT: One of the two Pipers at Boleigh (Bolleit) Farm. (WT)
RIGHT: St Buryan church, from an old engraving. (CCL) CENTRE: The
Dons Meyn at Roslucombe Farm. (WT) BELOW: Clarice de Bolleit's
tomb in St Buryan church, by J. T. Blight.

54

ABOVE: The sylvan beauty of Lamorna Valley, (CCL) and BELOW:
Lamorna Gate. (DM, VTP)

55

ABOVE LEFT: John E. Jackson of St Buryan, with a penny farthing bicycle almost as tall as himself, c1880. (WEC) CENTRE: Lamorna, with its pier for shipping off granite, by R.T. Pentreath. BELOW LEFT: St Buryan Methodist Sunday School about 1897. (WEC, SAG) ABOVE RIGHT: The *Lady of the Isles*, built at Hayle by Harvey's in 1875, struck the rocks at Lamorna Cove on 1 September 1904. Passengers and crew were saved, and the badly damaged vessel was refloated and towed into Penzance. (PHM, G) BELOW: The wreck of the motor tanker *St Guenole* of Rouen, bound for Irvine from Nantes in ballast, at Penberth Cove on 1 November 1948. An LSA search party picked up one survivor, but eleven others were lost. (PHM, R)

ABOVE: Kemyel Mills, Lamorna. Derelict since 1921, the wheel was restored and put to work again in 1978 by Nelson Hosking, Bill Carbis and Peter Ruthven. There was a mill here as early as 1300. (DT) BELOW: Rustic bridge, Lamorna. (AE)

St Levan

It has been claimed, with justice, that St Levan surpasses every other parish in Cornwall for bold and romantic scenery. To the east, the rugged granite headland of Trereen Dinas — formerly, as its name implies, a fortified cliff castle — thrusts itself proudly into the Channel, its summit crowned by a succession of small tors. Within this point lies Porthcurno with its white beach, and on the opposite cliff top, the unique open-air Minack Theatre presents plays staged against a spectacular natural backdrop. St Levan church nestles in its lonely valley beyond, while further west is the singular headland called Tol-pedn-Penwith, 'the holed headland in Penwith', where the collapse of a cave roof has formed a funnel in the cliff above.

St Levan (properly St Selevan), whose name the parish bears, was a brother of St Just. He figures in many folk tales, like the one connected with the St Levan Stone, a rounded boulder broken in two which lies in the churchyard. St Levan often used to rest here after one of his frequent fishing expeditions. Desiring to turn this rude but favourite seat into a memorial of himself, one day he gave it a blow with his fist and cracked it through. He then prayed over the rock and uttered the following prophecy:

'When with panniers astride
A pack-horse one can ride
Through St Levan's Stone
The world will be done.'

Happily, the opening in the rock has shown no recent sign of widening.

Among the ancient bench-ends in St Levan church is one depicting two fish caught on a single hook. This illustrates another story about St Levan; he once caught two chads on his fishing line, and not considering them dainty enough for some expected guests — his sister St Breage with two children — he threw them back, but they came repeatedly to his line until in the end he took them home. The children were ravenously hungry after their long walk, and not taking time to pick out the bones, were both choked. Ever afterwards St Levan fishermen called the chad 'chuck-cheeld' (choke-child). On another occasion, St Levan was crossing Rospletha stile towards his fishing place below the church to catch his dinner, when a woman called Johanna, who was collecting pot-herbs in her three-cornered garden, lectured the holy man for fishing on a Sunday. They came to high words, and St Levan told her there was no more sin in taking his dinner from the sea than she herself committed in taking hers from the garden. He called her 'foolish Johanna', and vowed that if another of her name was christened in his well, she would be a bigger fool than Johanna herself. From that day, no child called Johanna was ever christened in St Levan, all parents desiring to give that name to their daughters taking them to Sennen to be baptised. The path from St Levan's hut at Bodellen by Rospletha to St Levan's Rocks is said to have grown greener wherever he trod than any other part of those fields.

59

In Porthchapel Valley are some remains of the well, hermitage and chapel of St Levan. The churchyard cross is also said to be St Levan's; others are on the lychgate wall, at Rospletha, on the church path to Sawah and at Trebehor. There is also supposed to have been a Chapel-Curnow at Porthcurno, but the building depicted as such by Blight was dismissed by Henderson as 'nothing but a cow-house'.

St Levan church was a chapelry to the Royal Deanery of Buryan from at least the time of the Conquest. The present 15th century church incorporates portions of an earlier Norman building and comprises a nave, south aisle and north transept, with a western tower.

In his *Antiquities of Cornwall,* Dr William Borlase asserted dogmatically, writing of the Logan Rock poised on Trereen Dinas, that 'the extremities of its base are at such a distance from each other, and so well secured by their nearness to the stone which it stretches itself upon, that it is morally impossible that any lever or indeed force (however applied in a mechanical way) can remove it from its present situation'. Many years later, these words were construed as a challenge by Lieut. Hugh Colvill Goldsmith, RN, commander of the revenue cutter *Nimble,* who resolved to throw down this huge boulder, computed to weigh around 90 tons, from its lofty pedestal.

Accompanied by a dozen of his men, he went to Treen on 8 April 1824, and by repeatedly applying their united strength they caused the rock to 'log', or rock to and fro, so violently that it slid from its base and fell — fortunately in the direction opposite them. The great boulder did not fall into the sea, but lodged in a narrow fissure which stopped its descent. Lieut. Goldsmith — a nephew of Oliver Goldsmith, the playwright — found himself at the centre of a storm of public fury when news of his act of vandalism spread, and fears were even entertained for his life. However, Davies Gilbert, then in London, felt sorry for the foolish young man and interceded on his behalf; he persuaded the Admiralty to send down lifting gear from Plymouth, and himself raised a subscription of £150 to help defray the cost of replacing the rock. Their Lordships nevertheless insisted that the officer must carry out the work at his own expense or lose his commission.

Fittingly enough, Lieut. Goldsmith was placed in charge of the operation, and on 2 November, 'in the presence of thousands, amidst ladies waving their handkerchiefs, men firing *feux-de-joye,* and universal shouts, Mr Goldsmith had the satisfaction and the glory of replacing this immense rock in its natural position, uninjured in its discriminating properties'.

But the rock has never since logged so satisfactorily. Lieut. Goldsmith may have gained some glory by puting it back in its place, but he obtained no further advancement in his career, and died at sea off St Thomas, in the West Indies, on 8 October 1841, financially ruined by an act of folly which has paradoxically gained him a degree of immortality.

ABOVE: St Levan parish church, (DT) and BELOW: St Levan's Stone,
which will foretell the end of the world. (MF, WT)

61

ABOVE: Replacing the Logan Rock at Treryn Dinas, 2 November 1824.
(DT) BELOW: A dramatic impression of Treryn Dinas from Porthcurno.

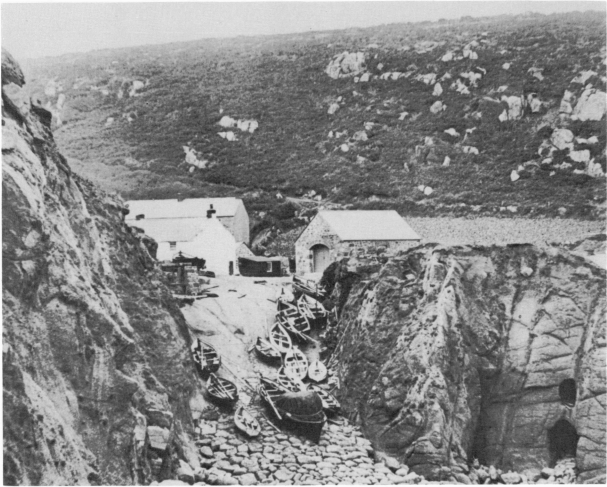

ABOVE: Porthcurno Valley in 1910, (PHM) and BELOW: Porthgwarra.
(CRO, FF)

63

ABOVE: Boats moored in Porthgwarra Cove, (CCL) and CENTRE:
Penberth Cove. (WEC) BELOW: When the ferro-concrete hulled schooner
Esperanca (built and owned by Preben Peterson of Denmark) drifted
ashore at Porthgwarra Cove on her return from Brazil in August 1977, she
was refloated by the united efforts of about 100 locals and holiday-makers
after salvage experts had given up. She was brought into Penzance for
repair. (WT)

Sancreed

There is some doubt as to the identity of the saint after which this parish is named. The principal claimants are St Credan, the disciple of St Petrock, whose remains are interred at Bodmin, and St Credan, son of Illadhan, who after sojourning in Cornwall settled in County Wicklow, Ireland. Nicholas Roscarrock, the 17th century Catholic hagiographer, recorded a tradition at Sancreed that the latter Credan by misfortune killed his own father, and was so moved by the tragedy that, abandoning the world, he became a hogsherd, his exemplary life causing him afterwards to be esteemed a saint. This had a curious echo more than a thousand years later. The parishioners of Sancreed instituted proceedings in the Consistory Court in 1667 against John Smyth, their vicar, alleging that in his sermon on Whitsunday (when the parish feast was celebrated) he had declared himself to be 'the unhappiest of ministers for that other ministers were pastors of their flocks but that he was but the herdesman of a company of swine and that he had lived amongst the Sancredians a great while and that he found them to bee but a company of hogg-drivers — saying "they love hoggs well and some of them will have a piece for their dinner — I wish them a good stomack" and then said that their saint was but a hogg-driver.'

Brennan's Castle, probably dating from the Iron Age, crowns the 652ft Caer Bran. Close by, at Chapel Uny, is an ancient village, with one of those mysterious underground passages known as fogous . Other prehistoric villages were at Hewes Common, Gold Herring and Bodinnar, while the Bronze Age menhir known as the 'Blind Fiddler' stands at Trenuggo.

A chapel was founded near a holy well, which probably bore the name of St Sancredus, at Chapel Downs. The well lies beneath the chapel, reached by a flight of steps from outside the south wall. On the western limits of the parish was the famous holy well of St Uny, for which many remarkable cures were claimed. Dr Robert Hunt relates that on the first three Wednesdays in May, children suffering from mesenteric diseases were dipped in this well three times 'against the sun' and then dragged three times round it on the grass, in the same direction. The chapel of St Uny, formerly near the well, has now quite disappeared. Other chapels existed at Bosence and Sellan, and the parish has many crosses, including two fine ones in the churchyard, with further crosses or cross-bases at Brane, Lower Drift, Trenuggo Hill and Sellan.

In 1182 Sancreed church was given by William, Earl of Gloucester, lord of the manor of Binnerton and Connerton, to the Priory of St James at Bristol, a cell of Tewkesbury Abbey; but in 1242 it was transferred to the Dean and Chapter of Exeter. The benefice, at first a rectory, became a vicarage in 1300. Nothing is known of the first church built on the site; of the second, an Early English building dating from the 13th and 14th centuries, only the short, massive western tower, the font and a few other fragments remain; the present church dates from the 15th century and consists of chancel, nave, south aisle and north transept. It was restored by J. D. Sedding in 1881-91. The church has been vested in the Dean and Chapter of Truro since 1889.

During the early and mid-19th century, when Gear Brane, Boswarthen, Wheal Argus, West Ding Dong and other mines were active, Sancreed churchtown was a lively little village with its own bowling green, butts and hurling ground, where the miners amused themselves in idle moments. Opposite the church was the Bird-in-Hand inn, now a farm, its sign depicting a hand holding a pheasant. Kathleen Hawke, whose family lived there and farmed the Glebe Farm, once asked her father how it was that the church and the local pub were invariably close together, to which he replied that it was probably owing to the thirst after righteousness.

A distinguished son of Sancreed was George Grenfell, Baptist missionary and explorer of the Congo, who was born in Ennis Cottage in 1849. The Royal Geographical Society published his chart of the Congo basin and awarded him its Founder's Medal in 1887. In 1891 the King of the Belgians and Sovereign of the Congo State presented him with the insignia of Chevalier of the Order of Leopold. He died of fever at Basoko on 1 July 1906.

A notable event of more recent times was the opening on 16 June 1961 of the new Drift Dam by the Rt Hon Henry Brooke, MP, Minister of Housing and local Government. It forms a reservoir supplying a considerable proportion of the water used in West Penwith.

Sancreed Church School about 1938. (R)

66

ABOVE: Sancreed church before 1910, (AO) and BELOW: a meet at the church. (DM, VTP)

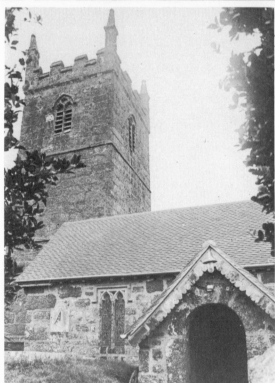

ABOVE: The rescue of survivors of the *New Commercial* of Whitby, wrecked on the Brisons Rocks about a mile SW of Cape Cornwall on 11 January 1851. Captain George Davies, RN, of the Penzance coastguard, and Mr Forward, commander of the Revenue cutter *Sylvia*, both received the RNLI Gold Medal for bravery. (ILN) BELOW LEFT: Sennen parish church, (MF, WT) and RIGHT: the headless figure of the Virgin Mary found in the church before restoration, *c*1700. (From the *Cornish Magazine*, 1899.)

Sennen

Sennen holds Cornwall's — indeed, England's — most famous topographical feature, the widely celebrated Land's End, and thousands of holidaymakers annually flock to this spot, attracted by the magic of its name. Yet just to the south lies a range of granite cliffs far exceeding in magnificence those at Land's End: Pordennack, Cairn Vean, Cairn Sperm, Cairn Evall, Cairn les Boel, Cairn Cravah and others, leading to Mill Bay or Nanjizel Cove, where the little stream divides this parish from St Levan.

The hamlet of Mayon takes its name from Table-Men, meaning Rock Table, a large flat stone at which seven Saxon kings are said to have dined together. Hals names them as Ethelbert, fifth king of Kent, Cissa, second king of the South Saxons, Kingills, sixth king of the West Saxons, Sebert, third king of the East Saxons, Ethelfred, seventh king of the Northumbers, Penda, ninth king of the Mercians, and Sigebert, fifth king of the East Angles, who all flourished about the year 600. Merlin, the wizard, added a rider to this unlikely tale with his prophecy that an even larger number of kings will assemble around Table-Men before some great event, or the destruction of the world itself.

St Senan, born near Kilrush in Ireland, reputedly founded a church on the present site in AD 520, afterwards sailing to Brittany to establish another. The 7ft high churchyard cross may have been used by him as a Preaching Cross before his church was completed. A small 13th century cruciform church eventually replaced the original structure and was enlarged in 1430, when the south transept was removed and the pillars and south aisle added.

On 21 February 1430, Pope Martin V issued a Bull to the Archbishop of Canterbury in response to a petition from the inhabitants of Sennen. 'They state that they have got Tower and Bells, and in the Church a Font. They begged the Pope to give them a licence to make a Cemetery around the Church. They said they could not accompany their dead to St Buryan lest their houses should be raided by pirates during their absence.' Sennen was included in the Royal Peculiar Deanery of St Buryan and remained a chapelry to Buryan until the last century.

The new section of the church was dedicated by Bishop Lacey of Exeter on 29 August 1441, the feast of the beheading of St John the Baptist. An inscription on the foot of the font stone commemorates the event: '*Haec Ecclesia in decollatione Sancti Johannis Baptistae dedicata fuit Anno Domini Millesimo CCCCXLI*'. Part of a mediaeval wall painting survives at the east end of the south aisle, depicting the New Jerusalem with a bridge going from earth to Heaven. In 1700 the sexton showed the historian Hals some headless figures recently found in the walls of the church, all curiously wrought and painted with gold, vermilion and blue bice on parts of their garments. Only one remains — the Virgin Mary — and new heads of the Mother and Child have been modelled by Mrs Sheila Hicks of Tregiffian.

Until the Reformation, a chapel known as Chapel Idné was the first building on the right on the steep hill down to Sennen Cove, and there appears to have been another ancient chapel at Penrose.

The manor of Hornwell, or Castle Hornwell, was chiefly located in Sennen. It seems, says Henderson, to have been given — probably by Duke Ordgar or King Ethelred — to the latter's foundation of Wherwell Abbey in Hampshire, from which its name derives, and to be identical with the Exeter Domesday manor of Witestan (Whitesand). The seigniorial rights attached to Hornwell manor extended over most of the coastlands between Land's End and St Ives.

It was from Whitesand Bay that Athelstan set out to subdue the Scilly Islands after his great victory at Boleigh. King Stephen landed here on his first arrival in England, as did the unsuccessful pretender Perkin Warbeck in 1497, although another account has it that he came ashore at St Ives. King John also landed at Sennen when returning from Ireland. Dr Robert Hunt records a curious tradition concerning the 'Hooper' or 'Hooter' of Sennen Cove. This spirit took the form of a band of misty vapour stretching across the bay, so opaque that nothing could be seen through it. The Hooper's appearance was invariably, and often suddenly, followed by a severe storm, and it was regarded as a kindly warning to fishermen. However, one old fisherman refused to heed it. The weather on shore was fine, 'and the aged sinner, declaring he would not be made a fool of, persuaded some young men to join him. They manned a boat, and the aged leader, having with him a threshing-flail, blasphemously declared that he would drive the spirit away; and he vigorously beat the fog with the "threshel" — so the flail is called. The boat passed through the fog and went to sea. A severe storm came on. No one ever saw the men or boat again; and since that time the Hooper has been rarely seen'.

The little harbour at Sennen Cove affords the only possible shelter on a long and terrible stretch of coastline, and a lifeboat has been maintained here since 1853. Despite launching difficulties — the lifeboat cannot put to sea for an hour and a half each side of low water — some gallant rescues have been performed by these boats. The breakwater at Sennen was erected in 1908, mainly through the exertions of Col. H. W. Williams of St Ives, to provide some shelter for the launching place. During the wreck of the ship *Khyber* at Porthloe Cove in February 1905, the lifeboat could not be launched because the seas were head on to the slip; as a result, 23 of the 26 people on board lost their lives. The *Susan Ashley* (1948-72) was launched on service 87 times, saving 64 lives and helping to save five others, as well as towing eight boats to safety. Her successor, the *Diana White*, which arrived in 1973, is a 37 ft Oakley self-righting vessel admirably suited to the difficult conditions at Sennen.

Building the breakwater at Sennen Cove, *c*1908. (PHM)

ABOVE: Sennen Cove before the breakwater was built; the striped buildings were occupied by the Western Telegraph Company. BELOW: The lifeboat house and circular capstan house at the cove.

ABOVE: The First and Last Post Office in England. (AE) BELOW: The famous old Sennen lifeboat *Ann Newbon*, which remained in service from 1893 to 1922.

ABOVE: Sennen Cove at the turn of the century, and BELOW: in 1928.

ABOVE: Mullet seine shot at Sennen, and BELOW: the Cypriot vessel
Nefeli (1,500 tons) wrecked at Dollar Cove, Land's End, 5 November 1972.
(WT)

74

St Just & Pendeen

The parish of St Just occupies a long coastal strip bounded on the south by Sennen and on the north by Morvah, while to the east a range of high hills divides it from St Buryan and Sancreed. At Carn Gloose or Ballowal Cairn is an ancient entrance grave of complex design, covered with a mound of stones and earth. A Bronze Age barrow was constructed at Tregaseal, and a fine cistal barrow on Portherras Common. Only one of two stone circles on Botallack Common now survives. At Kenidjack was a cliff castle, and in addition to the *fogou* at Pendeen, another at Lower Boscaswell was excavated in 1954-5 and found to date from the 3rd to 1st centuries BC. Perhaps the most fascinating relic of early man is the celebrated Plen-an-Gwarry (Playing Place) situated off Bank Square, St Just. In this amphitheatre, 126 ft in diameter, open-air performances of miracle plays were enacted in the ancient Cornish language down to the 16th century. In Dr Borlase's time, the surrounding bank was still 7 ft high (10 ft from the bottom of the ditch) and the seats consisted of six steps 14 inches wide and one foot high, surmounted by a further step on top of the 7 ft wide rampart.

On the isthmus connecting Cape Cornwall to the mainland stood a Chapel of St Helen, described by Dr Borlase. It later became a cattle shed, and only a few fragments now remain. On Chapel Carn Brea — the last hill in England — a chapel built of loose unmortared stones surmounted a large burial mound of the same material. Hals says that the barrow was 15 ft high, above which the chapel rose another ten feet, 'well built with moor-stone and lime, with a window in the east, and a durns, or door, on the south of the same stones; the roof all well covered or arched over with large flat moor-stones, wrought with the hammer and strongly fastened together'. It was surrounded by the 'downfalls of many sparstone-stairs and walks, by which heretofore the people ascended to this chapel and diverted themselves with a full prospect of the contiguous country by sea and land — St George's Channel, the British Ocean, and the Atlantic Sea towards the Scilly Islands'. Tradition has it that this chapel was dedicated to St Michael and attended by a resident hermit, who maintained a beacon for the guidance of shipping. At Boscaswell there was a chapel with a holy well, which had a domed roof and provided an excellent supply of pure water.

There are several contenders for the honour of being the patron saint of the parish, and some of the surviving legends reflect unfavourably on the character of the unknown saint. William of Worcester stated that St Just was buried in this parish, five miles west of Penzance on the coast of the far west corner of England — *'Sanctus Justus martir iacet in parochia Sancti Yoest distat a Pensans versus occidentem per 5 miliaria super litus occidentalissimae partis Angliae'* — but all trace of the church in which he was interred has long since disappeared. However, during the rebuilding of the chancel in 1834, the Vicar, the Rev John Buller, found an early Christian gravestone of the 5th century built into the wall by the high altar, inscribed with the Chi-Ro monogram and the words 'Sel(in)us (h)ic Iac(e)t' on the side and (possibly) 'Presbyter' on the base. A late 8th century cross shaft is built into the north wall, decorated with incomplete Celtic knotwork designs. Piers St Aubyn, who restored the church in the 1860s, cut 15 inches off its end because it projected across the window arch. He also discovered six mediaeval wall paintings, of which only two have been preserved.

On 13 July 1336, Bishop Grandisson dedicated the high altar of a new church, but only part of its chancel has survived, the present spacious and attractive building being mostly of the 15th century. The advowson belonged to the manor of Kelynack, but Sir John de Bello Prato (Sir John de Beaupré) gave it to Glasney College with the church lands of Lafrowda. The apportionment was confirmed by the bishop in 1355, and the college continued to enjoy the rectorial tithe until the Reformation.

The old St Just Market Cross was removed from the south-west corner of the churchyard to the vicarage garden by the Rev Buller, and afterwards thrown into the holy well of Venton East (in a field below the church) by his successor, the unpopular Mr Gorham. It was said of him in the parish that 'He don't love we and we don't love he'. The cross was found in the well, covered in mud and with the crucifixion downwards, by the Rev J. Andrewes Reeve, vicar 1882-93, and now occupies almost its original position.

The parish contained several ancient manors. Brea was a Domesday manor, at one time occupied by a family of that name. Botallack, the house built in 1665, was owned by the Usticke family, but in 1761 passed to the widow of Admiral Boscawen; other old houses included Trewellard (now demolished) and Bosavern. Pendeen manor was the residence of the distinguished Borlase family, who later moved to Castle Horneck, near Penzance. John Borlase was MP for St Ives in 1708, and of his two sons, the Rev Walter Borlase, LLD, a noted opponent of John Wesley, became Vice Warden of the Stannaries, while the Rev William Borlase, LLD, is remembered as the author of the *Antiquities* and *Natural History* of Cornwall. He also held the living of St Just in plurality with Ludgvan. Adjoining the house, with its gateway leading into a delightful Green Court, is a celebrated *vau* or underground passage.

In 1846 a new Peelite district was established to serve the area previously known as North St Just, including the ancient hamlets of Botallack, Carnyorth, Trewellard, Pendeen, Boscaswell, Calartha, Portherras and Bojewyan. This marked the inception of the new parish of Pendeen, of which the Rev Robert Aitken was appointed first vicar in 1849. A wooden church, built with the help of miners in the Square, where there was later a school playground, opened for worship on St John the Baptist's Day, 24 June 1849. Wood from this temporary building was used in the flooring of the permanent church, which was opened on 1 November 1852 and dedicated by Bishop Phillpotts of Exeter on 17 May 1854. Robert Aitken was his own architect and Pendeen church was built entirely by local labour, of stone quarried on the Carn at the back and brought to the site by farmers' carts.

St Just is a granite country of windswept, treeless farms and bleak, cairn-crowned moors, but on the western seaboard the granite is overlaid by a narrow band of greenstone. The contact zone between these two rocks is highly mineralised. Leland said that at St Just, alias Justini, there 'ys no thing but a Paroch Chyrch of [(?) and] divers sparkeled [scattered] Howses, the North Part ys Montaynes and Baren Growne, but plenteful of Tynne'. Although tin streaming was carried on at St Just from early times, deep mining did not become important until the 18th century, when adits were driven on the veins of ore outcropping in the cliffs. John Wesley and his brother Charles exercised great influence among the miners of St Just and Pendeen, John Wesley's visits spanning the years 1743 to 1789. One of their favourite preaching places was the Plen-an-Gwarry, where as many as 2,000 people would assemble to hear them.

During the 19th century the industry developed on a considerable scale: Levant, Botallack, Wheal Owles, Balleswidden and other mines each employed many hundreds of workers. In some cases, as at Levant and Botallack, the workings extend for some distance under the sea. The great depression, which affected mining from the 1870s onwards, brought much hardship to St Just, most of the mines being closed and many miners and their families compelled to emigrate to America and South Africa. However, Geevor remains in active production, and the industry's prospects appear bright.

The great annual day of celebration for the St Just miners — and indeed, for the entire parish — has traditionally been the Feast. This was originally observed on 13 July, the anniversary of the church's dedication, but in 1536 it was transferred to the Sunday nearest All Saints' Day (1 November) to avoid interference with the hay and corn harvest. It is still kept as a public holiday, but like most of the old customs, has lost something of its former spirit and character.

St Just parish church. (DJMJ, WT)

ABOVE: Pendeen parish church. (DJMJ, WT)   BELOW: Trewellard manor house, built 1641, demolished 1959. John and Charles Wesley were entertained here by John Bennetts. (M)

WRECKERS

At the Cornwall Quarter Sessions for Michælmas 1837,

BEFORE

E. W. W. PENDARVES Esq. M. P. Chairman,

AND A FULL BENCH OF MAGISTRATES;

THOMAS ELLIS aged 28 (son of Thomas), and THOMAS ELLIS aged 24 (son of Peter) both of the North part of the Parish of St. Just, who were committed by JOHN SCOBELL, Esq. on charges of Felony and Misdemeanor, for Plunder and Riot, at the wreck of the French Brig LE LANDAIS, at *Boscriggan*, on the 1st and 2nd of October were tried for the Felony, of which the elder prisoner was acquitted, and the younger found guilty. On the elder Prisoner entering into recognisances for future good behaviour, Mr. PEARCE, the prosecutor, consented to withdraw the second charge against him for Riot.

In pronouncing sentence on the younger Prisoner, the Chairman addressed him in the following words---

"THOMAS ELLIS,—I deeply regret to see so respectable a young man as you appear to be, with so good a character as many have spoken to, hold up your hand at that bar for so henious an offence as that which you have been convicted. You have been found guilty, and most properly so, by a very attentive and considerate jury, of plundering property from the wreck of a French vessel, which was cast on shore at St. Just. I am sorry that in your neighbourhood this has not been sufficiently regarded as an offence of the blackest dye. This infamous system of plundering from the unfortunate, has been too long a stain on our County; but you and all shall see that the magistracy of this County will at all times, render their utmost assistance in blotting out that stain, by bringing to justice and severely punishing all who are base and wicked enough to perpetrate these lawless and disgraceful acts of plunder. Instead of lending your aid in the protection of that property, which every manly and proper consideration would direct you to, you and your confederates have rushed into acts of plunder and destruction. It was not enough in your estimation, that the helpless should have experienced the misery of shipwreck, but you even attempted to strip them of the little which remained after all their other misfortunes."

"From the accounts we have of the extensive depredations committed on the cargo, and on what remained of the vessel, on the day preceding that on which you were detected carrying off some of the stolen property, we are induced to believe that many others have been much more guilty than yourself, and I only regret that they are not brought to that bar, to receive a far more severe punishment than that with which we shall visit you."

"The Jurors and the Prosecutor have recommended you to mercy. You have to thank them for their consideration, as well as those who have spoken to your former good character—and amongst them has been a most respectable magistrate of the County, who has known you for some years. But for this, the extreme sentence which we are enabled to pass upon you would have been inflicted, and your punishment would have been heavy indeed. If any one is brought again before this court for a similar crime, they must expect no mercy."

"Though the quantity of property you stole was of little value in itself, yet the enormity of the offence is great; your punishment however, compared with your offence, will be slight."

"It is hoped that the sentence will have its due effect, and that instead of rushing in numbers for the commission of acts of plunder, you and your associates will in future hasten to the protection of the lives and properties of those unfortunate beings who may be wrecked on the dangerous shores of our coast.— The sentence of the court is, that you, THOMAS ELLIS, be imprisoned in the Gaol of this County, for six calendar months, and during that time, that you be kept to hard labour."

This Address made a deep impression on the whole court.

PENZANCE, October 20th, 1837.

Resolved on all occasions to do my utmost to put down the nefarious system of plunder at Wrecks, I have thought it right to publish the foregoing excellent address, as a proof of the determination of the Magistrates of the County. Honest Salvors will continue to receive from me liberal and prompt Rewards; but lawless plunderers shall most certainly be brought to punishment.

RICHARD PEARCE, Agent to

ROWE, Printer, Bookseller, &c. Penzance.

A warning notice to wreckers, issued following the wreck in fog of the French brig *Le Landais,* carrying a valuable cargo of brandy, wine, cotton and tobacco, at Boscregan on 1 October 1837. It was plundered by miners and country people. The poster was discovered during the renovation of a shop in Fore Street, St Ives, in 1963. (M)

ABOVE: Priest's Cove, near Cape Cornwall. (PHM) BELOW: Pendeen
House, birthplace of Dr William Borlase. (M)

80

ABOVE: A charming view of Cape Cornwall from the Rev Buller's *Statistical Account of ... St Just*, 1842. BELOW: Levant Mine *c*1850, by W. Willis, of Penzance. (CCL)

81

ABOVE: The Crowns section of Botallack Mine, from a painting, (DRC) and BELOW: restoring the collar of Wheal Cock in 1907, about the time that the mine began its last unsuccessful phase of working. (CCL)

82

The Prince and Princess of Wales (later King Edward VII and Queen Alexandra) descending the famous submarine incline shaft at the Crowns section of Botallack mine, 24 July 1865. (ILN)

ABOVE: Market Square, St Just. On the right is the horse 'bus run by Ben Eddy, outside his Wellington Hotel; its modern competitor, owned by the Great Western Railway Company, is on the left. (PHM) BELOW LEFT: The St Just Feast, (R) and RIGHT: the first GWR 'bus on the St Just to Penzance route, driven by W. C. Bolton. (PHM)

Morvah

The austere moorland parish of Morvah, on the north-western seaboard of the Penwith peninsula between Pendeen and Zennor, contains much unspoiled hill scenery, particularly at Carn Galver, while the cliffs below, including a magnificent series of granite pinnacles rising to 400 ft, are perhaps the most impressive in Cornwall.

On the high moors south of Morvah church are the ruins of an exceptionally large and strongly-built Iron Age fortress known as Chun Castle. It has been dated to the 3rd century BC, and its inhabitants knew how to smelt both iron and tin. It consists of two concentric stone walls; the inner has a diameter of 174 ft and a thickness of 12 ft and was once 10-12 ft in height. The outer wall, separated from it by a ditch, is 230 ft in diameter. The entrance was by a causeway protected by a curtain wall and a deep bottle-necked inner gateway. A short distance away stands the much older and still perfect Chun Cromlech.

Morvah has been a chapelry to Madron since the parish was formed, and it first appeared as a separate fiscal unit in the Subsidy Roll of 1327. On 7 May 1390 the Vicar of Madron had licence to celebrate Divine Service in chapels of the Blessed Mary and of Saints Bridget and Morvetha in his parish: *'in capellis beate Marie de Laneyn necnon Sanctarum Brigide et Morvethe infra parochiam suam situatis'*, provided the mother church suffered no prejudice. Henderson interpreted this as meaning that two chapels were licensed, the second being called after SS. Bridget and Morvetha and referring to Morvah. However, at Tregaminion, in a marshy field north of the church, near the cliff, are slight remains of an ancient chapel and well which may have been dedicated to St Morwetha. Near the well is a rock known as the Giant's Stone, around which Morvah people used to dance. A chapel of St Bridget in Madron was licensed on 22 September 1400, and on 17 April 1409 Richard Reche, chaplain, had licence for a chapel of St Morwetha, but could not administer the sacraments without the vicar's permission.

'Morvah' means 'place by the sea', and it has been suggested that St Morwetha was a mediaeval fiction derived from this name. St Briget (Brigid or Birgitta) of Sweden lived from 1302 to 1373, and founded the Monastery of Vadstena in 1344, as well as an order of nuns known as Brigetines. Her canonisation process began in 1378, at about the time the Knights of St John of Jerusalem built the church of Morvah. Their building consisted of an aisle arcade of three bays and a tower. In 1447 Bishop Lacey of Exeter granted an indulgence of 40 days to all persons visiting or supporting 'the chapel of St Brigida in the Parish of St Madron'. Because of the connection with St Brigid, the Swedish community in Britain and the community of Vadstena have recently become interested in Morvah church. In 1972 the feast day of St Briget in Cornwall was changed from the Sunday nearest 19 October to 8 October, to conform with the celebration of her festival in the rest of the world.

Both Charles and John Wesley were extremely active at Morvah, despite the bitter opposition of the Rev Walter Borlase. On 25 July 1744 Charles prayed over the foundations of the Society's House here. This later became the Sunday School attached to the chapel, built in 1867 and subsequently bought by the Bryanites.

In 1828 the dilapidated church was rebuilt, except for the tower. The opening service took place on Friday 17 October, when the sermon was preached by the Rev C. V. Le Grice; the following Sunday, the speaker was the curate, the Rev H. Penneck. On both occasions the church was crowded, and the singers of the mother church in Madron joined in rendering the Coronation anthem. Mr Le Grice composed a hymn for the occasion which contained an allusion to the church's exposed situation:

> 'The winds may roar, the tempest frown,
> Each breast from fear is free;
> The worshipper looks calmly down
> Upon the troubled sea.'

It was at Morvah church — not at Zennor, as is often said — that 'the cow ate the bell-rope'. This story was the subject of a poem published in 1865 by 'Cornubian West' (J. Morgan Anthony, Postmaster at St Ives). In the dead of night the sexton, parson, clerk and parishioners were roused by the untimely tolling of the church bell, and hastened to see what was amiss.

> 'They went through the churchyard, the parson before,
> In his hand he carried a light,
> When lo! when they came to the belfry door
> Out bolted a monster with terrible roar
> And they all started back in affright.
>
> The parson he tumbled right heels over head
> O'er the clerk who was close in his rear,
> For he hindered his progress as backwards he fled
> Though parsons have no business with fear.
>
> His hat and his wig both went by the board
> And a gust of wind blew them away;
> And as it passed by, it maliciously roared
> At the head of the parson who wished he had snored
> On his pillow till dawning of day.'

Some thought the intruder a ghost; others believed it to be the devil — a view which seemed to be confirmed when the bell-rope was seen to have disappeared and a cloven hoof mark was found by the belfry door. Eventually, the nocturnal campanologist was identified as simply a hungry cow attracted by the straw rope in the tower — for Morvah is a hungry parish.

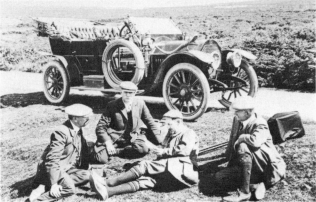

ABOVE: An 'iceberg' in glass engraved with the outline of Morvah church, presented to the church in 1972 by Eskil Wilhelmsson, Swedish manager of the Dartington Glass Works, Torrington. (WR,WT) BELOW: A motoring party pulls in to the roadside near Bosigran in 1906. (CCL)

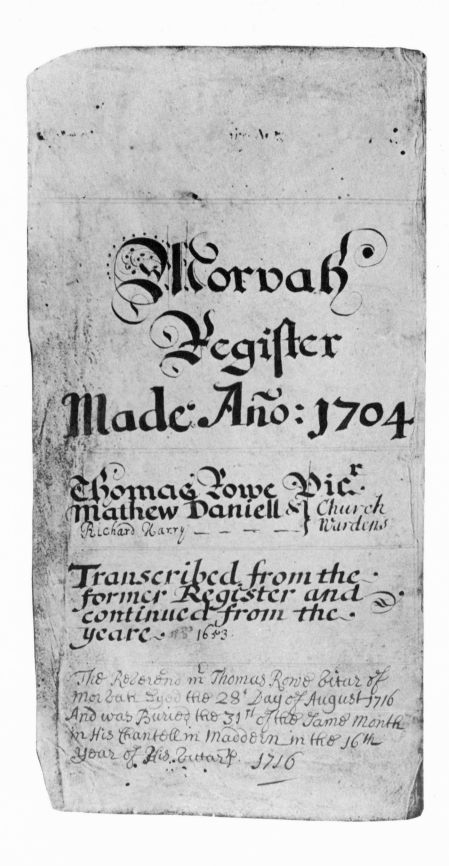

Title page of the earliest surviving Morvah parish register. (WR, WT)

St Ives

West of St Ives lies the wild moorland parish of Towednack, named after St Winwaloe; its only centre of population is at Nancledra, in a deep valley some distance from the church, which stands on a remote windswept site near Amalveor and Beagletodn Downs. Still further west is Zennor, whose patron saint is the female St Senara. It is a parish of high hills and moors, but with a fertile plain dividing them from the sea, and hence known as 'the land flowing with milk and honey'. The district is completely unspoiled, and Zennor village, with its background of brooding hills, is a place of great charm. In the church is an old carving of the mermaid who, attracted by the sweet singing of young Matthew Trewhella in the choir, enticed him away to live with her beneath the waves in Pendour Cove.

St Ives itself takes its name from the Irish St Hia or Ia, a sister both of St Herygh, patron of St Erth, and of St Uny, who established himself at St Uny Lelant, on the western side of the Hayle estuary. Lelant was already a place of importance by the 13th century, having both a market and custom house, but silting of the river led to its loss of trade to St Ives, which developed during the 15th century into a busy little market town and seaport.

The fishing industry was once important, especially pilchard seining, which was conducted on an extensive scale in the sandy shallow coves between Porthgwidden and Carrack Gladden. Mining also played an important role in the local economy, particularly during the last century; the largest mines were concentrated in the Stennack Valley, at Carbis Bay and around Trencrom and Trink hills. The village of Halsetown was built in the 1830s by James Halse, MP, to house his miners.

In 1558 St Ives was created a Parliamentary borough, sending two members to Westminster; the number was reduced to one in 1832. Charles I granted the town corporate status in 1639, and this lasted until 1974, when the Penwith District Council was established. St Ives still has a Town Mayor and Town Council.

The earliest known engraving of St Ives, by J. Farington, published 1 May 1813. (CCL)

ABOVE: Tregenna Castle with a distant view of St Ives. (From the Tregenna Sale Catalogue, 1871.) BELOW: Abbey Hill, Lelant. (DT)

ABOVE: The slate memorial in Lelant Church to William Praed of Trevetho (d. 1620). He is depicted with his wife and children, and the inscription reads: 'Think gentle friend that now dost view this tomb Tomorrow must thou go to thy last home.' (GBW, WT) BELOW: Church Road, Lelant. (M)

ABOVE: House boats on the beach by Lelant Ferry. The pylons which carried the power supply across the river have now been replaced by a submarine cable. (CT) BELOW: Zennor churchtown *c*1880. (JBDC, WT)

ABOVE LEFT: A memorandum in a Zennor register by vicar Jacob Buller, warning against being imposed upon by parishioners bringing tithes in kind to the church. (JBDC, WT) RIGHT: The top of Fish Street, (RIC, EA) and BELOW: the rear of Halsetown Inn, with pump in the foreground. (LEC)

ABOVE LEFT: Bailey's Lane, 1900; Robert Uren with cart and Mrs
Paynter with Annie and Loveday Paynter on the porch. (M, LEC)
BELOW: Children on Smeaton's Pier; Wood Pier is in the background.
(PQ) ABOVE RIGHT: Cleaning ray in St Ives harbour, (M) and BELOW:
unloading bricks from a damaged vessel in the harbour. (RIC, EA)

ABOVE: Seine boats at Porthminster. The pole in the foreground marks
the boundary of the stem. (RIC) BELOW: Carbis Bay station, 1920. All
these buildings have now been destroyed. (CCL)

ABOVE: SS *Lyminge* wrecked at Gurnard's Head on 19 September 1931. The 2,500 ton London registered vessel, bound from Cardiff for Oporto with coal, came ashore in thick mist. The crew landed at a cove under Gurnard's Head Coastguard Station. (G) BELOW: The wreck of the schooner *Enterprise* of Beaumaris on Lelant sands, 11 September 1903. Bound from Charlestown to Manchester with china clay, she came ashore on the Western Spits during a fearful gale and her crew of three men and a boy were rescued by the St Ives lifeboat *James Stevens 10* under Coxswain Stevens. (G)

ABOVE: A group of mineworkers, mostly carpenters, at Giew Mine (St Ives Consolidated Group). (BS, SAG) BELOW: Trenwith Radium Mine, St Ives, *c*1912. (CCL)

ABOVE: Zennor school in 1912. (R) BELOW: The St Ives Primitive
Methodist Chapel Choir in the early 1900s. (R)

BACK ROW: Mr French jnr, Mrs Fleming (nee Phillips), H. Trevorrow, G. B. Thomas, Mrs Thomas (nee
Chard), J. Q. Cocking, Miss Lander, W. Thomas, William Trevorrow. MIDDLE ROW: Mat Thomas, Mrs
Toman (nee Trevorrow), Mrs Kemp (nee Berriman), Mrs Major (nee Lander), Mrs Peak (nee Beard), Mrs
Jennings (nee Freeman), Mr French (choirmaster), Miss Mary Carbines, Mrs Vaughan (nee Trevorrow), Mrs
Uren (nee Ninnis), Mrs Lugg (nee Uren). FRONT ROW: Mrs Stevens (nee Couch), Mrs Couch (nee Uren), Mrs
Sisley (nee Couch), Miss French, Mrs Farrell (nee Hart), Mrs Lethbridge (nee Harry), Mr Beard, Mrs Cocking
(nee Chard).

98

Gwinear

Gwinear, the most easterly parish in Penwith, contains several traces left by early man: there were ancient fortifications at Gear and Coswinsawsen, and encampments at Reawla and Drannack. The presence of the Romans is attested by the discovery of some of their coins at Trungle and Coswinsawsen.   The parish takes its name from St Gwinear, one of the band of Irish missionaries whose eponyms are so plentifully scattered around the St Ives Bay area. From the *Life of St Guigner* written by Anselm, a Breton monk, around the year 1300, it appears that Gwinear was the son of an Irish king, Clyto, his Irish name being Fingar. St Patrick converted him to Christianity, whereupon his heathen father banished him. Accompanied by his sister Piala and some nobles, he set out for Brittany, where he lived in a cave as a hermit and also founded a monastery. As St Guiner, he is patron of the parish of Languengar, while at Pluvigner, near Auray, he had a chapel, cross and well. He later returned to Ireland, by then Christianised, but refused an offer of kingship.

With a large party, Fingar again sailed for Brittany, but was carried by the wind to Cornwall. Landing at Hayle in AD 455, he and his 777 followers came to a town called Conetconia, after which the ancient manor of Conerton, in Gwithian, is named. The legend tells that a faithful woman called Coruria stripped the thatch from the houses to provide the saints with bedding, and killed her only cow so that they might have food. Having eaten and said grace, Fingar ordered the cow's bones to be collected and the skin placed on them, then asked his companions to pray. They did so — and the cow stood before them alive, and fairer than before. Fingar drank some of her milk, praying that she might yield three times as much as other cows. This privilege was granted, and extended to her progeny.

The party met with quite a different reception from Tewdrig, the local pagan chieftain, who (according to Leland) lived at Riviere in Phillack, for he at once pursued them. Fingar and a companion had gone ahead to spy out the land and came to a valley where, being thirsty, he drove his staff into the ground and brought forth a copious stream of clear water. Meanwhile, Tewdrig fell on the main body of the invaders — for that was probably how he regarded them — who were then resting on a hillside, and put them all to the sword. Hearing their cries, Fingar hurried to the scene, where Tewdrig beheaded him with a single stroke. According to Anselm, the saint did not die immediately, but carried his head to the hilltop, where two quarrelling women so enraged him that he cursed the spot, that it should thereafter bring forth nothing but scolds. He turned aside to a beautiful fountain and washed his head, then returned to the site of the massacre which, when Anselm wrote, was divided from the well by a small wood. Here, Fingar sank to the ground and expired. The spring which issued from the spot where he had been beheaded still flowed in Anselm's time near the tree which grew from his staff. Fingar and his companions were buried by a countryman named Gur, and over the saint's body a church was later erected.

The chapel and well are believed to have been at Roseworthy. No trace of the church now remains, but the well has been identified as Gwinear Well, near the farmhouse; its waters are reputedly beneficial as an eyesalve. The most splendid Celtic cross in Cornwall also stood at Roseworthy, but during the 18th century it was removed to Lanherne Nunnery, Mawgan in Pydar. It was made in the 7th or 8th century. Another early cross was discovered in 1954, built into the wall of the vicarage. Only the damaged head remains, but the figure on it is still intact.

The patron of St Gwinear church was the Bishop of Exeter. In 1311 Sir Reginald de Beovyle (Beville), lord of the manor of Drannack, later re-named Herland, transferred the advowson with an acre of land to Sir Richard de Stapledon. He gave it to the Chapter of Exeter in trust for his brother's, Bishop Stapledon's, foundation at Oxford, known as Exeter College. The great tithes were to maintain twelve poor scholars in the University.

A few fragments of the earlier Norman church remain, and the east window is of the 14th century, but the present large church of St Gwinear dates from the 15th century. The tower was still under construction in 1441, for Michael Lercedekne, treasurer of Exeter Cathedral, left 40s by his will of 5 January of that year towards the tower or purchase of bells for the church of 'Sancti Wynneri'. The early 16th century aisle or chapel on the north side was erected by the Arundells of Roseworthy.

John Wesley recorded, in his *Journal* for 15 September 1760, particulars of the great storm which, beginning at Land's End between nine and ten at night on 9 March 1759, 'went eastward not above a mile broad, over St Just, Morvah, Zennor, St Ives and Gwinear, whence it turned northward over the sea ... It broke down the pinnacles of Gwinear church, which forced their way through the roof. And it was remarkable, the rain which attended it was salt as any sea-water.'

Roger Williams, the apostle of religious freedom, was born at Gwinear on 21 December 1602. After graduating from Pembroke College, Cambridge, in 1624, he left for New England in 1629. Among the best known of local families were the Lanyons of Lanyon. Captain William Lanyon, RN, was the last survivor of the officers who sailed twice round the world with Captain Cook, and was with him when he died. Other notables were the Polkinhornes of Polkinhorne, the De Coswyns of Coswin (Coswinsawsen) and the Pennecks of Taskus.

Gwinear is essentially an agricultural parish, but it once possessed a considerable mining industry. The Rosewarne and Herland mines were noted for their silver production. Herland, usually called the Manor, gave a large enough return to Mr Hoblyn, part proprietor only of the land, to pay for the building of Nanswhyden House in St Columb Major around 1750. A 70 inch pumping engine was erected on Herland as early as 1758, and by 1814, according to Carne, the mine had sold about 156 tons of silver.

Gwinear Road station in 1935; on the right, the Helston branch line, which opened 9 May 1887 and closed 3 November 1962. The station has now been completely destroyed. (CCL)

ABOVE: Gwinear parish church, (RJE, WT) and BELOW: the thatched
Roseworthy Methodist Chapel, closed 1975. (WT)

ABOVE: Old cottages at Roseworthy. (CT) BELOW: Carnhell Green.
(DT)

ABOVE: The Roseworthy Arsenic Works. (CCL) BELOW: South Parbola, alias Wheal Jennings, a tin mine 1¼ miles ESE of Gwinear. The picture probably dates from about 1908. (CCL)

103

ABOVE: St Gothian's Chapel, Gwithian, for many years buried beneath the sand. (PHM, G) BELOW: The former Hundred Pound of Conerton in 1890. Surrounded by trees and marsh, it was used for impounding stray cattle. (CT)

Gwithian

Gwithian parish fringes the north-eastern corner of St Ives Bay, and the greater part of it lies buried under sand, blown in from the beach by prevailing westerly winds. Its patron saint is St Gothian, whose name underwent a transformation in the 16th century to Gwythyen. Little is known of him, but he appears to have been one of the band of Irish missionaries who landed at Hayle in the 5th century, only to be slain by Tewdrig.

Gwithian was the site of the great manor of Conerton, the paramount manor of Penwith, and also of a considerable town of the same name. Before the Conquest, the manor of Conerton belonged to the Honour of Gloucester — it has even been suggested that it comprised the ancient principality ruled by Tewdrig. Its owner, Britrics, Earl of Gloucester, when on a visit to Normandy, jilted Matilda, the Conqueror's future wife; she never forgot the insult, and after years obtained her revenge — and her faithless suitor's manor of Penwith. On her death it passed to Robert Fitzhamon, and in 1154 Robert, Earl of Gloucester, gave the manor to Richard Pincerna, whose grandchild married into the Arundel family of Lanherne, who held it for a long period. The Arundels were ruined by the Reformation because of their Catholic sympathies; and this once influential and extensive manor degenerated into a mere nominal possession.

Gwithian parish, a chapelry to Phillack, originally bore the name of the manor. In the 12th century William, Earl of Gloucester, gave all the Cornish churches in his fee to the Priory of St James, Bristol, among them *'ecclesiam de Conorton et ecclesiam de Eglasheil* [Phillack]'. This grant was confirmed by Henry II, but the advowson of both parishes nevertheless remained attached to the manor.

John Leland's two accounts of the district, written in 1538, make interesting references to the lost town: 'By Conarton cummith a river, cawllid Dour Conor [Conor Water, that is, the Red River], and goith into the Se not far from Lanant [Hayle] Ryver Mouth. In the Mouth of the Ryver that cummith by Lanant ys the Rokket [Rock] Godryve, whereyn bredeth Se Fowle.' 'Nikenor [Conerton], a 2. Myles from Ryvier, sumtyme a great Toun now gone; 2. Paroche Chirchis yet seene a good deal several [separated] on from the other, sumtyme in the Towne, but is now communely taken to be in S. Guivian's Paroch, and ther cummith a Broket [Brook] to the Sea.'

The position of Conerton has been established by the study of local place names, combined with archaeological excavation and aerial photography. It lay just north of Gwithian churchtown, its centre probably under the present village green, and extended under the sand dunes and along the line of Sandy Lane, where recent wind erosion has revealed buried fields, rubbish heaps containing sea shells, ash and bones, and large quantities of pottery dating from the 10th to 13th centuries. The former Hundred Pound of Conerton still survives, a circular embanked enclosure lying south-east of the church and adjoining the green. It was used for impounding stray cattle, which could be claimed on payment of a fine.

Prof. Charles Thomas suggests that the site was first occupied by a wooden oratory during the 6th or 7th centuries and then by the first stone chapel, erected during the 7th or 8th centuries. After this was engulfed by sand, a second stone chapel was built over it in the late 9th or 10th centuries. This building apparently consisted only of a nave, a chancel with altar and benches being added at the eastern end during the late 10th, or 11th century. The chapel was probably abandoned owing to further incursions of sand during the 13th century, when it was replaced by Gwithian parish church, dedicated to St Gothian. A simple cruciform structure, this underwent considerable enlargement during the 15th century, the main additions being the fine western tower and a south aisle.

The parish church was one of the buildings mentioned by Leland, the other the older chapel to the north, still partly visible. By Dr Borlase's time (1750) it had disappeared under the sand, but it was rediscovered in 1827 when Richard Hockin, of Churchtown Farm, set his men to dig a pond to be supplied by the small stream — Leland's 'Broket' — which runs northwards from the green to the bridge over the Red River. They uncovered the chapel's eastern wall, together with some skeletons, and Mr Hockin — 'a practical Methodist' — had the building dug out and converted into a cowshed.

The parish church underwent some modification in the 18th century, and extensive restoration in 1865 was necessitated by the deterioration of its soft sandstone and killas (slate) walls. Edmund Sedding, the architect, restored the building to its original plan of nave, chancel and two transepts. The cost was borne almost entirely by the Rector of Phillack, Frederick Hockin.

Gwithian possesses one of the only two thatched Methodist chapels in Cornwall. (The other is the now disused Roseworthy Chapel, on the A30.) The little building, part stone, part cob, is tucked away at the rear of the Pendarves Arms Hotel. Built in 1810, it was opened on Sunday 24 February 1811 by the Rev Mr Collier with prayer and an appropriate sermon (based on Psalm V, 7) to a crowded congregation. The interior fittings were renewed in 1959, and in 1969 the chapel was re-thatched by Sid Williams and his son John. It was one of the first chapels in West Cornwall to hold an annual harvest thanksgiving service.

A dangerous reef called The Stones extends a mile seaward from Godrevy Island off the coast of Gwithian. Many disastrous wrecks have occurred here, including that of a ship carrying the executed Charles I's wardrobe to France in 1649, and a lighthouse was established on the island in 1859. The Red River, which falls into the sea at Gwithian, has for centuries drained numerous mines in the Camborne area; it derived its name from the refuse brought down suspended in its waters. A little mining was caried on at Gwithian itself, the workings including Wheals Emily, Nanterrow, Nancemellin, St Andrew and Liverpool.

But Gwithian is principally a farming district, overwhelmed by hillocks and dunes of shifting sand, to which much good agricultural land has been lost. Mr Hockin told Lysons (who wrote in 1814) that his great-grandfather remembered how the barton of Upton, one of the principal farms, was nearly buried in one night, the family making its escape through the chamber windows. During the winter of 1808-9, having disappeared for more than a century, the house came into view again when the wind shifted the sand. The sandhills formerly supported a small local breed of sheep, whose mutton possessed a superior flavour derived from the tiny conical snails which live on the short grass of the towans.

106

ABOVE LEFT: Gwithian parish church, (RJE, WT) and RIGHT: an
aerial view of Godrevy lighthouse, designed by James Walker and built by
Thomas Eva of Helston. It was first lit on 1 March 1859. (CT) CENTRE:
Gwithian, with the lighthouse just visible in the distance. (CT) BELOW:
The steamer *Nile*, which was wrecked off Godrevy in 1854. (ILN)

ABOVE LEFT: The Gwithian Methodist Society had the right of stabling for the horse of any visiting preacher, during services, in the yard and stables of the Pendarves Arms Hotel, adjoining the chapel. The horseman shown here is believed to be Mr Jenkin, the last preacher to exercise the right. (CT) RIGHT: The thatched Methodist chapel. (WT) BELOW: Connor Downs School in 1914. (R)

Phillack

The original undivided parish of Phillack included most of the present town and port of Hayle, which in Cornish signifies river. The name Phillack is less easy to explain. Prof. Thomas claims that its meaning is unknown, but Henderson, perhaps wishfully, derives it from Piala or Ciala, the sister of St Fingar. A small glass phial, discovered during the 19th century restoration of the church, is thought to have contained the blood of the saint. During the Middle Ages, confusion over the names led to the dedication of the parish church being transferred to the more orthodox Felicitas, and both saints are now recognised as patrons.

Evidence of early Christianity in the parish is clustered around the church. The lychgate crucifixion slab is described by Prof. Thomas as 'something almost unique, a pictographic memorial stone of the Celtic period, which must have remained ever since it was first set up, in this same little enclosure'. An early Chi-Rho stone in the gable over the south porch cannot be later than AD 450, and hints at Christian influence in this part of Cornwall prior to the arrival of Fingar and his companions. A similar indication is afforded by the celebrated inscribed stone now erected in the little park of Carnsew at the western entrance to Hayle, near where it was discovered in December 1843. In 1891 the Rev William Jago gave its now illegible Latin inscription as 'HIC PACE NU (PER) REQUIEVIT SILVANUS CONIUX CUNAIDE HIC IN TUMULO IACIT VIXIT ANNOS XXXIII': 'Here in peace lately went to rest Silvanus, husband of Cunaide. Here in the tomb he lies. He lived for 33 years'. In the churchyard is a tall, wheel-headed granite cross dated at c1000, while against the wall of the old vestry stands an inscribed stone pillar reading 'CLOTUUALI MOBRATTI', apparently signifying '(the grave of) Clotuuali (the son of) Mobratti'.

A cruciform Norman church which once occupied the site was apparently adapted to form the transept of its 15th century successor. The present church is essentially a Victorian edifice. It dates from a 'restoration' of 1856-7, when virtually the entire 15th century building, except the tower, was demolished and rebuilt in an enlarged form to serve a greatly increased population.

In 1870 a new parish was created from the western portion of Phillack, and appropriately named St Elwyn. When the Irish saints arrived at Hayle, they divided into two groups. One, led by Fingar, moved eastwards to Conner, and was massacred by Tewdrig; the other, under St Breaca (patron saint of Breage) with St Elwyn, moved south up Hayle River and secured possession of the fort on Tregonning Hill, which controlled the surrounding district, returning later to avenge Fingar's death. The new church of St Elwyn was built in 1886-8 by John Sedding, the eminent Victorian church architect; it was his last work. A chapel-of-ease has also been provided at Copperhouse and a mission room at Conner Downs.

John Wesley first preached at Hayle on 14 September 1765. On Saturday 27 August 1785, he wrote: 'About nine I preached at the copper-works, near the [River] Hayle, in the new preaching-house. I suppose such another is not in England, nor in Europe, nor in the world. It is round, and all the walls are brass, that is brazen slags. It seems nothing can destroy this, till heaven and earth pass away.' This curious little building stood in Fore Street, and was made of black blocks of slag from the copper smelting works which gave Copperhouse its name. Despite Wesley's prediction, it did not last, for it became redundant when a new and larger chapel was opened at Copperhouse in 1817; converted into a house and shop, it was demolished in the 1820s.

Methodist chapels were also built at Foundry (1845), Angarrack (1834 and 1873), Ventonleague (1875), Highlanes (Bible Christian) (1869) and Wheal Alfred. The Teetotal Methodists had a chapel at Mount Pleasant, while the former Baptist chapel (1874) has now become a Roman Catholic church. A modern central Methodist church has been opened at Hayle in recent years to replace the large Copperhouse and Foundry chapels.

The industrial history of Hayle began in 1758, when a copper smelting works, established at Camborne four years earlier, moved here to save the heavy cost of transporting materials by road. Previously, Cornish copper ore had been sent by sea to Swansea for treatment. The opening of a Cornish smelter hardly made economic sense, since it took three times the quantity of coal to smelt any given weight of copper ore, whereas sending the ore to Wales brought the advantage of return cargoes. However, through the outstanding abilities of John Edwards, a protégé of Dr William Borlase, the enterprise prospered; even today, the vast amounts of black slag still to be seen in the district, some cast as building blocks and incorporated into walls and buildings, testify to its scale. The Cornish Copper Company also began importing coal, timber, limestone, iron and other goods into Hayle.

In 1779, John Harvey, an enterprising blacksmith from Carnhell Green, Gwinear, established a foundry at Hayle to make cast iron pumps for the mines; he also engaged actively in trade, thereby earning the enmity of the older concern. On 7 November 1797 Jane Harvey, daughter of John, was married at St Erth church to Richard Trevithick, the great Cornish inventor, and a few years later (1800-1) the parts for his famous steam road carriage, precursor of all forms of mechanical transport, were cast for him at Hayle Foundry.

John's son Henry — the 'great Mr Harvey', as he was called — inherited the foundry in 1803. As both he and the Copper Company sought to develop and improve their respective sections of the harbour, hostility between the rival concerns reached new heights of bitterness, involving boundary disputes, physical confrontation and legal action. John Edwards built a dam with sluice gates across the eastern arm to keep back the water at high tide; released some hours later, it swept silt and sand from the channel and kept the river clear for navigation. Henry Harvey built quays and wharfs, together with his own sluices, supplied by water impounded in the artificially created Carnsew Pool. Affairs reached crisis point in 1818, when the Copper Company sought to prevent Henry Harvey from constructing a new quay, hundreds of workmen being deployed as 'troops' by both sides and an actual clash only narrowly averted. The Copper Company also entered into direct competition with Harvey's in another sphere, by opening its own foundry for the manufacture of machinery, including some fine beam pumping engines, for the mines. The long-running conflict, which divided Hayle into two warring camps, was not finally resolved until 1867, when the Copper Company — then Sandys, Carne & Vivian — sold out to Harvey's, which thereby gained sole control of the harbour.

In 1845 Harvey's built the world's largest pumping engine, with a 144 inch cylinder, for draining the Haarlem Mere in Holland. Harvey's also built a number of ships at Hayle, ranging from small sailing ships to steamers of considerable size. The closure of the foundry (though not of the firm) in 1904 was a tragedy for the district.

Several mines were worked in the Hayle district, the most famous being Wheal Alfred, a mile and a half south of the town. This was one of the richest copper producers in the county. In 1824, two large steam engines were installed here, one a 90 inch single and the other a 40 and 70 inch compound. On the Black Cliff, half a mile north of Phillack church, was Wheal Lucy, while on the eastern margin of the sand dunes lay Phillack Towans or Loggans mine. In Angarrack valley, close to the railway, was Mellanoweth mine, otherwise Wheal Maggot. Angarrack also possessed an interesting smelting house, said to be the first used by Becher and other Germans for smelting tin ores in reverbatory furnaces by coal. According to D. B. Barton, it was established by Francis Moult & Co in 1704, with six of these new furnaces.

Industries connected with mining were also represented in the area. Towards the end of the last century a dynamite works came into operation at Hayle Towans, while the long-established firm of J. & F. Pool, manufacturers of perforated metal sheets, still provides valuable employment in the town. The convenient port facilities available at Hayle led to the opening of a coal-fired electric power station in 1911; its recent closure, with the consequent loss of coal traffic, has jeopardised the commercial future of the harbour.

During the last century, Hayle became an important communications centre. In 1825 a causeway across the river estuary greatly shortened the former route by road around St Erth to Penzance and St Ives, also avoiding the dangerous crossing of the sand at low tide. A steam packet service to Bristol was inaugurated in 1831 by the steamer *Herald,* while a few years later (1834) Parliament sanctioned the construction of the Hayle goods and passenger railway, which linked the port with the mining district around Redruth. The station lay at the foot of the present Foundry viaduct, and trains were drawn up the steep incline at Angarrack by a stationary engine.

A lifeboat station was established here in 1866, the first lifeboat, donated by Oxford University Colleges, being named *Isis.* The boats of this station saved the crews of many vessels stranded in the vicinity of Hayle Bar. The station closed in 1920, and the area is now served by the St Ives lifeboat.

Fore Street, Copperhouse. (DT)

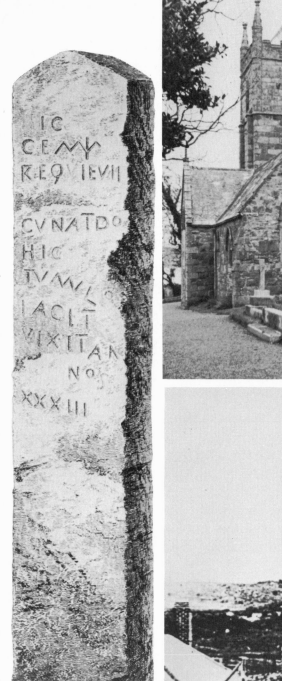

LEFT: An inscribed stone at Hayle, from Richard Edmonds' *The Land's End District*, 1862. ABOVE: Phillack parish church, (RJE, WT) and BELOW: Wheal Lucy on Hayle Towans, whose adit opens at the south-western end of the Black Cliff. It produced tin in the 1870s and 1890s. (CCL)

112

ABOVE: The inaugural launch of Hayle's first lifeboat, the *Isis*, at Oxford in 1866. (ILN) BELOW: The last lifeboat is named the *Admiral Rodd* on 31 August 1907. The boat was presented by Mrs Rodd of Tunbridge Wells in memory of the late admiral. (CT)

ABOVE: Hayle Regatta, 2 September 1905. (DT) BELOW: Harvey's foundry, Crotch's White Hart Hotel, the *Cornubia* horse 'bus, and the original Hayle Railway Station at the foot of the present viaduct, *c*1845.

114

ABOVE: A Hayle street scene about 1910, (CCL) and BELOW: Foundry
Square in the same period. (CCL)

115

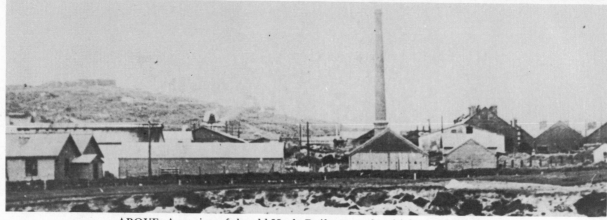

ABOVE: A portion of the old Hayle Railway track, which ran along the main road from Foundry Square to the swing bridge and then along the north side of the canal. (CT) CENTRE: A compound engine built at Hayle Foundry. (CRO) BELOW: The dynamite works of the National Explosives Company of Upton Towans, which once employed 700 people. A terrible explosion in January 1904 killed four workmen and injured many more, also causing widespread blast damage in Hayle, St Ives and Lelant. (CCL)

St Erth

Situated at the head of the Hayle estuary, St Erth was the site of Roman occupation. At Bosence is what has been described as a perfect Roman entrenchment; articles of Roman workmanship were found here during the 18th century, and described by Dr Borlase in his *Antiquities of Cornwall* (1759 edition). Another less perfect Roman fortress lies on a hilltop near the St Erth bridge.

The church and parish of St Erth took their name, like so many in Penwith, from an Irish saint, in this case St Erc (or Ercus) son of Deagh. He was the only one among the courtiers of King Laoghaire to rise from his seat when St Patrick entered the king's presence. Patrick baptised him when he was an old man and made him the first Bishop of Slane. He joined the group of missionaries which included his sister St Ia and his brother St Uny, sailing on up the Hayle to a site then known as Lanuthnoe. This name, still borne by the churchtown lands, suggests a yet earlier dedication to a St Uthinock, the prefix 'lan' signifying a monastery. The alternative name of Lanuthnoe was long retained for the church. St Erc died in 514, aged 90; his festival is kept on 2 November and observed on the nearest Sunday to All Saints' Day.

During the 12th century a boundary dispute between the parishes of Lananta (Lelant) and Lanhudna was submitted to the Pope for arbitration. The Precentor and Chancellor of Wells, deputed to adjudge the matter, decided that the disputed lands, namely those of 'Gunhen' situated below the main road which led from 'Cruce Aldrou' straight to the sea to the south, towards 'Trelewid' (Treloweth), should thenceforth belong entirely to the parish *'beati Erchi de Lanhudna'*. Bishop Bartholemew (1159-84) confirmed the award.

All that remains of a Norman church at St Erth is a font bowl, discovered beneath the Lady Chapel floor during restoration. Around 1199 the church belonged to the Bishopric of Exeter, but Bishop Henry granted the Chapter of Exeter a pension of two silver marks from the church of Lanuthinoch, with the reversion of the whole church on the death of the then vicar, Herveus. In this way the church became appropriated to the Dean and Chapter some time before 1237.

In 1331 thieves entered the chancel by the windows and stole the chalice, books and wax. Galfridus, Vicar of St Erth a few years later, appears to have been somewhat pugnacious, for he was indicted of beating and wounding Reginald Eir of Trewelisek (Trelissick) at St Erth on the Monday after All Saints' Day in 1350, and of beating Robert Thenge, servant of William Botriaux, at Boswithgy (Bosworgey) on the Monday after St Mary Magdalene in 1357.

There were then several chapels and shrines at St Erth. About the year 1260, a Sir William de Roscrou, lord of the vill of Boswoedki (Bosworgey), was granted the right of a chantry in the Chapel of the Blessed Mary Magdalene by the Dean and Chapter of Exeter, on condition that he paid yearly *'in signum subjeccionis'* a pound of wax for the high altar of the parish church, promising also to maintain a priest to serve the chapel and to repair the fabric. Henderson states that it was the earliest licence for a chapel in Cornwall and showed what elaborate precautions were taken before domestic chapels became widespread. On 6 December 1406 Henry Gurlyn and his wife Margaret had licence for a chapel, presumably at Gurlyn, their residence. There were also chapels at Porthcollumb, Trevessa (1403), Trewinnard (1372), Treloweth (1379), Trelissick (1418), Treven and Rose-an-Grouse. A fine cross at Treven was removed in 1906 to St Michael's Mount for preservation, and another at Tredrea (Park-an-Grouse) to Trelissick in Feock.

The present parish church, a pleasing building, enhanced by its sylvan setting, is mostly of the 15th century, with some excellent Perpendicular work, but the tower and possibly the chancel go back to the 14th century. The parish registers commence in 1563 and the church also preserves a copy of Charles I's letter of thanks to the Cornish people for their support during the Civil War. On the triumph of the Parliamentary cause, Mr Whiteinge, then vicar, was ejected from the living, and an illiterate replaced him. The vicar in 1747, Mr Collier, in an excess of Protestant zeal, caused the mediaeval stained glass and 'sentences' (texts) painted on the walls to be destroyed. In 1779 George Rhodes, vicar of Lelant, stated: 'I reside at St Erth, of which I am also vicar, and have a curate who serves Lanant and Towednack and lives in the town of St Ives'.

Major Herbert Carter, VC, son of a former vicar, the Rev C. R. D. Carter, is buried in the churchyard. The company he commanded during the Jidballi campaign in Somaliland was driven back by a troop of Dervishes who outnumbered them thirty to one, leaving behind a badly wounded Indian sepoy who had lost his horse. Major Carter rode back alone 400 yards, charged the Dervishes, and after three attempts got the wounded sepoy on his own horse and brought him to safety. He died of fever in East Africa at the beginning of the Great War, while preparing to attack the enemy.

In a drastic restoration of the church in 1874 some portions were completely rebuilt. The Trewinnard Chapel on the south side, part of which is said to have belonged to the manor of Trewinnard, was reconstructed in 1912 and a new screen added by Mrs Hawkins, widow of Christopher Hawkins of Trewinnard and Probus.

The manor of Trewinnard gave its name to an ancient family, that of the De Trewinnards, who are said to have flourished here even before the Norman Conquest. According to Hals, Deiphobus Trewinard in a fit of anger 'killed an innocent man and buried him secretly in Trewinard Chapel, of public use before the Church of St Earth was erected'. The coroners of the shire, learning of the crime, opened the grave, removed the body and empanelled a jury, who brought in a verdict of wilful murder against Trewinard. He was then sent to Launceston Gaol to await trial. To save his life, he entered into an arrangement with Sir Reginald Mohun, a favourite of Queen Elizabeth, transferring to him all his estate on condition that Mohun used his influence with the queen to obtain a pardon if he was condemned. Trewinard was condemned at the next Cornish assizes and sentenced to be hanged, but Mohun, who had secured a reprieve in advance, put it into the Sheriff's hand, and Trewinard was soon released. Thereafter, he lived on a small pension allowed him by Sir Reginald out of his own now forfeited estate.

Trewinnard later became the property in turn of Sir Thomas Arundell, Sir Nicholas Hals and the Hawkins family. Sir Christopher Hawkins, who also owned Trewithen, achieved some notoriety as a 'borough-monger' by his brisk trading in Cornish 'rotten boroughs' during the early 19th century. It was in Trewinnard that the famous coach with leather straps in place of springs, now displayed at the County Museum, Truro, originated. Built around 1700, it was last used by the Hawkins family in 1780. Around 1782 the Cornish Copper Company of Hayle constructed a mill on Trewinnard land for rolling copper and iron, but the enterprise eventually failed, like the copper smelter, because of the cost of transporting coal.

Trelissick was once the seat of the Paynter family. It was on 7 October 1715 that James Paynter with other Cornish gentlemen, proclaimed the Old Pretender King James III at St Columb Major. The Jacobite movement was not strong in Cornwall, and failed mainly through the initiative of Hugh Boscawen of Tregothnan, who called out the militia. Paynter was tried at Launceston, but acquitted, and on his way home was 'welcomed with bonfire and bell from Launceston to the Land's End', probably a tribute to his personal qualities rather than to his opinions. His mother was a Miss Sutherland, of Scottish origin, which was probably the reason for his sympathy with the Pretender.

At Tredrea lived Davies Gilbert, the celebrated Cornish historian, collector of carols, 'discoverer' of Sir Humphry Davy and friend of inventors Sir Goldsworthy Gurney and Richard Trevithick. He was a Cornish MP for 30 years and succeeded Davy as President of the Royal Society. His widespread activities in so many fields earned him the title of the 'Cornish Philosopher'. He was actually born Davies Giddy, but took his wife's name of Gilbert.

The celebrated bridge of St Erth was said by Leland in 1538 to have been built 200 years earlier, before which there had been a ferry. It was certainly there in 1447, when John Trevelyan bequeathed 12d to 'Sanctus Ercus and his bridge'. The causeway is of some length, but originally the bridge had only three arches, a fourth and larger one being added later at the eastern end. The roadway was extremely narrow, so that damage frequently occurred to the walls from passing carriages, but in 1816 Davies Gilbert succeeded in getting it widened at a cost of over £100, of which he contributed more than half. 'Good talle Shippes' came up Hayle estuary before it was choked by tin refuse, and in 1750 Dr Richard Pococke described a proposed scheme for cutting a canal from St Erth to Mount's Bay, but as the river mouth would always be choked with sand and the ground was so high to the south as to make it an expensive undertaking, the idea was never implemented.

Henry Davies, Davies Gilbert's great-uncle, joined with others to start a tin smelting house at Treloweth in 1715. The crest of his arms, a lamb carrying a flag, was adopted as a mark for the tin slabs produced there. This device suggested to those in Catholic countries an idea of consecration, and they showed a preference for Lamb Tin, although it was no better than any other. As a result, all the Cornish smelters were obliged to adopt the same or similar marks.

LEFT: An ancient cross in St Erth churchyard, (GRW, WT) and RIGHT: the parish church. (GRW, WT)

119

ABOVE: Old cottages just south of St Erth station. (M) BELOW: Fore
Street, St Erth, (DT) and INSET: the memorial to Major Herbert Carter,
VC, in the churchyard. (GRW, WT)

St Hilary & Perranuthnoe

St Hilary church is dedicated to a fourth century Bishop of Poitiers who, after being converted to Christianity, became a powerful antagonist of Arianism. His day is kept on 14 January. A Roman milestone, discovered built into the chancel wall, bears the name of Constantine the Great. It apparently dates from AD 306-308. Several versions of the inscription have been given; but the Preb. Scarth's extended reading is generally accepted: 'Imperatore Caesare Flavio Valerio Constantino Pio Felice Invicto Caesare Filio Augustorum Divi Constantii Pii Augusti Filio'. Beside the churchyard path is another ancient inscribed stone whose significance is much less clear, bearing the mysterious legend 'NOTI NOTI' on one side. It is possibly a Romano-British sepulchral monument.

A religious edifice of some kind has probably been here since early times; the advowson and rectory were given in the twelfth century by a Lord of Trevarthian to the priory of St Michael's Mount, conditionally on his descendants enjoying a perpetual Corrody in the monastery and the monks entertaining four of their retainers, with their horses, greyhounds and sparrowhawks, at Christmas, Easter and Whitsuntide.

Trevarthian in this parish was of some importance during the Middle Ages, says Henderson, as the residence of the Trevarthian family, until they migrated to Merthen in Constantine following a marriage with the co-heiress of Carminow. At the 'vill of Trevarthyan' about the year 1375, John Browderer, king's sergeant-at-arms, with Roger Trewynnarde, attacked a priest called Sir Walter Sancre, and binding his arms behind him, cut off his head with a sword. The head set on a spear was carried publicly to London, as if it had been that of the vilest traitor, though Sir Walter was a man of good reputation. Both offenders were excommunicated for this serious crime.

Set on an eminence about two miles inland from Marazion and visible from both Channels, the 14th century tower of St Hilary church and its broach spire used to be kept whitewashed as a daymark for shipping. The 15th century church was destroyed by fire in the 19th century. No detailed description of it has come down to us, but it is known to have comprised a nave, chancel, two side aisles and western tower. It had a rood screen, removed at the Reformation, and the roof was of oak. The ceiling of the north aisle was decorated with carvings. Of the twenty stone pillars, those of the north aisle were cut from Godolphin Hill granite and moulded in the Norman style; the others, of stone quarried at Castle-an-Dinas and Trencrom, were plain octagonal columns.

William Godolphin, who married a daughter and co-heiress of Walter de Gaveregan, lived at Treveneague and died on 11 July 1589. His was the oldest monument in the church; it had a Latin inscription and verses, and the Godolphin family arms were cut in the stone.

During the Commonwealth period, the living of St Hilary was held by a Mr Palmer; ejected at the Restoration for not complying with the Act of Uniformity, he nevertheless continued to preach to his followers. For this he was committed to prison by the local magistrates, one of whom, Mr Robinson of Treveneague, the prisoner addressed in the prophetic words of Micah: 'If thou return at all in peace, the Lord hath not spoken by me'. Shortly afterwards, Mr, Robinson was gored to death by his own bull, a circumstance which excited no little wonder at the time.

Another rector of St Hilary, the Rev Malachi Hitchins, born at Gwennap around the year 1740, was distinguished both as mathematician and philosopher. When Dr Maskelyne, the Astronomer Royal, went to St Helena in 1761 to observe the transit of Venus, Mr Hitchins was given full charge of the Royal Observatory at Greenwich. He subsequently assisted Maskelyne in preparing the first Nautical Almanac, which appeared in 1767, a work invaluable to seamen the world over. He became rector of St Hilary in 1774, but continued his close association with the almanac until his death in 1809. One of his sons, Fortescue Hitchins, who lived at St Ives, assisted Samuel Drew in writing a history of Cornwall, and also published some poetry.

John Wesley visited St Hilary on several occasions. His fellow preacher, John Nelson, recorded in his *Journal* for 1743 that when he and Mr Wesley were returning from St Hilary Downs, where the latter had preached to the people from Ezekiel's vision of dry bones, Wesley stopped his horse to pick blackberries, saying: 'Brother Nelson, we ought to be thankful that there are plenty of blackberries, for this is the best country I ever saw for getting a stomach, but the worst that I ever saw for getting food. Do the people think we can live by preaching?'

The fire which destroyed the church on 26 March 1853 was started by sparks escaping from the sheet iron pipe of a small stove in the upper end of the chancel, which had rusted badly where it passed through the roof. On the previous day, Good Friday, two services had been held in the church; the small congregation huddled around the stove for warmth while a snowstorm raged outside. The alarm was raised about three in the morning by two young people from the village — a chorister and his brother — and a man from the neighbouring village of Goldsithney, who saw the flames from their bedrooms. The interior was already an inferno, and the roof of the chancel and north aisle had fallen in, while that of the south aisle blazed furiously, the flames fanned by a strong east wind. Everything that could burn was burnt — communion table, pulpit, pews, seats, with all their ancient oak carvings depicting the Passion and Crucifixion, singing gallery, and King Charles' letter of thanks to the Cornish people.

Said an eye-witness: 'As a sight . . . imagination could not picture any thing more awful. There it was in the dead of such a night, surrounded by tall and branchy elms clothed with snow, and venerable by age, burning in awful silence, like the vast funeral pyre of the countless dead that lay interred beneath the shadow of its walls'. Enginemen on the neighbouring mines observed the steeple bathed in an unusual light without suspecting the true cause, as it was full moon with a clear frosty sky. The tower, though suffering some damage, survived largely intact, while the snow that lay thickly on the buildings prevented the fire from spreading to the vicarage and houses nearby. The church was quickly rebuilt by architect William White on the same plan as before, incorporating much of the old stonework; the rededication took place in October 1855.

St Hilary attracted much public attention in 1927, when the vicar, the Rev Bernard Walke, presented a Nativity play, *Bethlehem*, acted by the villagers, which was broadcast by the BBC from the church itself. The unaffected simplicity of these performances — for the broadcasts continued for several years — made a lasting impression on all who heard them. Father Walke (whose ministry lasted from 1913 to 1936) was a controversial figure, and the Catholic practices which he introduced aroused the strong opposition of certain ultra-Protestants, who succeeded in having many ornaments and the stone altars removed from the building. However, it still contains much of interest and beauty — notably the pictures on the stalls, depicting scenes from the lives of Cornish saints, painted by Newlyn artists Harold Knight ARA, Norman Garstin, Alathea Garstin, Gladys Hynes, Ernest Proctor, Dod Proctor and Ann Walke.

St Hilary touches the sea in the vicinity of Prussia Cove. This took its name from the celebrated smuggler Capt John Carter who, when playing soldiers with his brothers as a lad, fancied himself as Frederick the Great, King of Prussia. In that secluded spot he, Capt Harry Carter and Capt Will Richards established their headquarters in the late 18th century, and in an artificial opening in the cliff called 'Channel Rush', a lugger would often creep inshore to discharge her cargo of kegs on the flat rocks. On one occasion the smugglers actually fired on the naval sloop HMS *Fairy* from a battery on the cliff between Prussia Cove and Bessy's Cove, but their guns were seized by a landing party while they made good their escape. John Carter also attacked the Custom House at Penzance and regained possession of some of his own brandy, which had been seized by the Revenue men. His brother Harry wrote the *Autobiography of a Cornish Smuggler*, which still makes fascinating reading. John eventually quit this adventurous life and settled quietly on a small farm at Rinsey, where he died in 1829.

Mrs Pascoe's *Walks Round St Hilary*, written between 1836 and 1846, come as a shock and a revelation to those who cherish the illusion that life in a remote country parish around 150 years ago was an idyll of contentment, peace and happiness. Mrs Pascoe was the wife of a vicar who ministered there for half a century, and thus had an excellent opportunity of studying local social conditions. The picture she paints is a grim one of almost unrelieved poverty and hardship. She refers to the 'Poor House' at Goldsithney and its wretched inmates; to parish pay of a shilling a week doled out to unfortunates who had to consent to be called 'paupers' before they qualified for it; to the ravages of 'fever' caused by lack of sanitation; to widespread drunkenness, miners blinded by blasting accidents underground and a young lad transported to Australia for committing a petty theft. In all this, St Hilary was typical of many parishes of the time, but few possessed as honest a chronicler as Mrs Pascoe.

The neighbouring parish of Perranuthnoe takes the first part of its name from St Piran, one of the two saints to whom the parish church is dedicated. The other is St Michael the archangel, possibly chosen because of the village's proximity to St Michael's Mount. The parish feast is kept on the Sunday nearest 5 March, St Piran's Day. The second part of the parish's name is derived from its paramount manor, Uthno or Udno (Odenol in the Domesday survey). During mediaeval times it was generally known as Uthno Parva; in 1311 the parish was referred to as St Pyeranus and in 1403 as Udno Peryn.

St Piran landed from Ireland at Perranporth, on the north Cornish coast, around 498, and built a small church near Perranzabuloe. Here he ministered until his death about twenty years later. This building, buried under the drifting sand during the ninth century, was rediscovered in 1835 and is said to be the oldest surviving Christian church in this country. St Piran crossed Cornwall through Perranarworthal and Perranwell to Perranuthnoe, and also carried the Gospel to Brittany. He is probably the best known of the Cornish saints, and taught the Cornish miners, whose patron he became, a new method of smelting tin; his emblem, a white cross on a black ground, has been adopted as the Cornish national flag.

Legend has it that St Piran's church at Perranuthnoe now lies beneath the sea, for certain old writers assert that at the time of the inundation of Lyonesse, a man on horseback was swept from Whitesand Bay in Sennen to Perran, through a sea which swallowed up a large area of land around Mount's Bay. The first known church on the present site dated from 1160. It had a small squat tower and a thatched roof. In 1740 it was enlarged to meet the needs of a growing population, the north transept being taken down and the present north aisle built in its place, while the tower was heightened to provide a landmark for shipping. The carved font, two Norman doorways and the south transept survive from the earlier building.

Sir Michael Tregorra, who was instituted as rector in 1427 and resigned in 1433, became the first Rector of Caen University in Normandy, which was founded by Henry VI in 1440. He also became chaplain to that king and in 1449 was appointed Archbishop of Dublin, dying there in 1471. His effigy in St Patrick's Cathedral was restored by Dean Swift.

The principal village of the parish is Goldsithney. On 12 September 1400 John Andrew, a layman, had licence to erect a chapel of St James in the village centre, but during the 18th century it fell into ruins, and it has now completely disappeared. The only surviving relic is a little stone effigy of St James the Great, set above the keystone of the south door of the parish church. Another ancient chapel once existed at Chapel an Crows, near Trevean.

Henderson states that in 1399 Goldsithney was called 'Pleyn-Goyl-Sithny', which may be translated 'Sithney Fair Field'. There is an old tradition that this fair, together with its name, was 'stolen' from Sithney near Helston by some Perran people, who ran off with the glove which was suspended from a pole as its charter. For years this glove was displayed at Goldsithney on St James's Day, the date appointed for the fair. The lord of the manor, as proprietor of the fair, paid a shilling a year in token acknowledgement to the Sithney churchwardens. Documentary evidence appears to confirm that the fair had already been transferred to Goldsithney as early as 1250.

A short distance inland from Cudden Point, John Shakspeare of Pendarves in 1775 built a mansion similar in design to Tregenna Castle at St Ives, and named it Acton Castle, after his wife's family name. The point projects boldly into the sea, commanding a magnificent view of the greater part of Mount's Bay.

SS *Ornais II* ashore at Perran, 6 December 1929. (PHM, R)

ABOVE: The obsolete warship HMS *Warspite* ran ashore at Mount Malpas Ledge on 23 April 1947. Penlee lifeboat rescued eight men. (PHM, R) BELOW LEFT: Perranuthnoe parish church, (RJM, WT) and RIGHT: the Noti Noti stone in St Hilary churchyard. (RJM, WT)

ABOVE: Rebuilding St Hilary church after the fire of 1853. (HH) BELOW LEFT: St Hilary Church; the 14th century tower and spire were possibly designed by a French architect from the Mount and built by local workmen. Note the filled in Cornish stile in the gateway, to keep stray animals from entering the churchyard. (RJM, WT) RIGHT: Smugglers' house, Prussia Cove.(PHM, G)

ABOVE: Nativity play at St Hilary church, directed by Father Bernard
Walke. (HH) BELOW: The Rev Bernard Walke. (HH)

127

ABOVE: Crowliss Stream, 1871, by W. J. Welch. (R) BELOW: Wall painting in Ludgvan church copied by Dr William Borlase in 1740.

Ludgvan

The parish of Ludgvan extends from the sand-fringed shores of Mount's Bay to the bleak uplands of Castle-an-Dinas, and embraces some rich agricultural land, together with the villages of Canon's Town, Cockwells, Crowlas, Nancledra and Ludgvan itself. As in other parts of West Cornwall, a sharp distinction has been made between the low-lying land near the sea, called the Morrep or Morrab (seaboard), and the higher ground to the west, called Guiendarn (moor part). The men from the Morrep used to play those from the Guiendarn at the traditional sports of hurling and wrestling.

Although the prefix 'St' has long been applied to Ludgvan, it does not appear in any version of the name earlier than the 14th century, and popular legends of a miracle-working Irish missionary notwithstanding, his actual existence is much in doubt. In his manuscript history of the parish, written in 1770, Dr Borlase derives Ludgvan from the Lyd stream or Marazion river; but it almost certainly originated from the important manor of Ludgvan Leaze (Ludgvan Court), mentioned in Domesday as 'Luduham', which extended into the parishes of Lelant, Towednack and St Ives. By 1230 this had become 'manerium de Ludwon', in 1279 'Leudvon', and in 1283 'Ludvon'. In 1290 the church was referred to as 'ecclesia de Ludewon', while the name of the saint first appeared in 1312 as 'Sanctus Ludwanus'. He would thus seem to be a mediaeval invention, possibly intended to bring Ludgvan into conformity with other 'sainted' parishes round about.

After the legendary St Ludgvan had erected his missionary church on top of the hill overlooking the beautiful waters of Mount's Bay, he knelt on the stile and prayed, and presently a pure crystal stream welled up through the dry earth. So the holy well of Ludgvan was established, and its water acquired a great reputation. In particular, all children baptised in it were supposed to be granted immunity from the hangman's hempen rope. The belief appeared to be well-founded, for over the centuries no native of the place was ever hanged, and Ludgvan people felt themselves absolutely protected from this fate. However, their confidence was rudely shaken when, on 12 August 1820, a Crowlas woman called Sarah Polgrean, aged 27, was publicly hanged at Bodmin for the murder of her husband, whom she hated. She was thought to have been born close by the well, and seemed almost certain to have been baptised in its water, in accordance with local custom. However, a diligent search showed that a mistake had been made over her birthplace: the register of her baptism was eventually discovered not at Ludgvan, where it was first sought, but in a neighbouring parish. It was clear that she could not have been baptised with water from Ludgvan well, whose unique properties, now fully rehabilitated, obtained more widespread celebrity than ever, bottles of it being taken to churches throughout the district and used by special request of parents for the baptism of their infants.

At Collurian Farm was a chalybeate well whose water was widely acclaimed as an eye-salve, and hundreds resorted there yearly to bathe their eyes, but it seems unlikely that this was a holy well. It has been destroyed by mining operations.

A small wedge-shaped granite slab bearing two incised granite crosses with exaggerated end bars, thought to be a 7th century Christian grave marker, was found in 1962 in the southern side of the churchyard. The Norman church erected at Ludgvan churchtown (called Ludewon-Eglos in the Assize Rolls of 1289) was cruciform in shape, but nothing of it remains except the font. One of the first incumbents, Alan de Bloyou, found it necessary on one occasion to avail himself of the sanctuary of his own church. In 1301 the jurymen of the Hundred of Penwith reported that he had slain Michael le Messegere in the town of Marcagou (Marazion). He took refuge with his brother Ralph, and both were ordered to be taken, but in the meantime Ralph had died under the *'peine forte et dure'* (had been pressed to death) for other crimes, while Alan had made good his escape.

Several mediaeval chapels existed in the parish. On 19 August 1387 James Gerveis had a licence for his chapel at 'Treyuwel' (Truthall), the site of which is now covered by mining refuse from West Wheal Fortune. A 'Chapel Tubinas' (St Thomas' Chapel) mentioned in 1395 stood on the north side of the main road between Whitecross and Canon's Town on Colurrian estate. There are believed to have been other chapels at Ludgvan Leaze, Trenowin and Treassowe. Seven Ludgvan crosses are recorded. Three are in the churchyard, with the beautifully decorated shaft of a fourth built into the tower stairs. There are more alongside the main road: one, painted white but lacking a shaft, gave its name to the little village of Whitecross, while the other, set in the hedge at Cockwells, has inscribed on its base 'Manor of Tregender'. Finally, a cross head may be seen built into the walls of Treassowe manor.

The chancel of the parish church was rebuilt early in the 14th century, and on 14 July 1336, Bishop Grandisson of Exeter re-dedicated the church to St Paul the Apostle. The magnificent tower and north aisle were constructed in the 15th century, the final addition being an enriched granite porch. In March 1740, masons brushing the church walls in preparation for reliming discovered a mediaeval painting of St Christopher surrounding the north door. Dr Borlase, the rector, made a copy of this curious picture, which was afterwards once more obliterated. Its most interesting feature was a representation (over the doorway) of a small chapel or chantry.

On 30 July 1771, a pinnacle was thrown down from the church tower by lightning; popular superstition assigned the cause to the vengeance of a perturbed spirit, exorcised from Treassowe, passing eastward to its place of banishment in the Red Sea. In an insensitive restoration in 1840, the porch was destroyed together with the south transept, to permit the building of the south aisle, stones from the porch being used to construct a lychgate. In 1912-13 a new vestry was added to the south aisle, which was itself rebuilt in granite in place of the former brick.

The most distinguished Rector of Ludgvan was Dr William Borlase, who held the living for half a century (1722-72). Born at Pendeen Manor on 2 February 1695, he was educated first at Penzance and Plymouth, and took his degrees of BA and MA at Exeter College, Oxford, in 1713 and 1716 respectively. Ordained in 1717, he became Rector of Ludgvan in 1722 and of St Just in 1732. Dr Borlase devoted much time to studying the archaeology and history of his native county, and set the seal of fame on his learning with the publication of three monumental works: *The Antiquities of Cornwall* (1754), *Observations on the Islands of Scilly* (1756) and *The Natural History of Cornwall* (1758). The University of Oxford conferred on him the degree of Doctor of Law in recognition of his life's work as an historian. He died in 1772, and was buried with his wife in the chancel of Ludgvan church.

The former influence of the manor of Ludgvan Leaze is shown by the fact that it held as appendages the advowson to the rectory of this parish, as well as the high lordship of St Ives, where certain dues were paid to the lord of the manor for ships entering the port, and where also, at the annual manor court, the corporation maces were borne before the steward. The manor was given by Richard, Earl of Cornwall, to the Ferrers family, from whom it passed, by successive heiresses, to those of Champernown and Willoughby (Lord Broke). Through a co-heiress of the latter it came to a Paulet and thus eventually to Henry Paulet, last Duke of Bolton, who died in 1794.

The ancient manor of Truthall (Treiwal in Domesday) was owned before the Conquest by the monks of St Michael's Mount, represented by Brismar the Priest. Half of it was seized at the Conquest by the Earl of Mortain, who gave it to Blohiu Brito, founder of the turbulent Cornish family of Bloyou. Varfell was occupied for a considerable period by the Davy family. In mediaeval times this estate was included in the demesne lands of the manor belonging to the Abbess of Wherwell in Hampshire, from which it apparently takes its name.

Treassowe (formerly Trewrasou) was for years the seat of the Rogers family, who afterwards moved to Penrose, near Helston; their old residence is now partly ruined. The 765 ft Castle-an-Dinas on this estate was crowned, as its name suggests, by an ancient fortress, which consisted of two concentric stone walls of great height and thickness, surrounded by a partially-built third wall. Already badly damaged in Dr Borlase's time, its destruction is now almost complete. In the late 18th century Mr Rogers of Treassowe used some of the stones to build a folly known as Rogers' Tower.

On the slope below was the grave of James Hosking, a Ludgvan farmer, who visited America in 1811 to study farming conditions and printed an interesting account of his experiences for private circulation among friends. Described as 'a very honest man, but of singular opinions and eccentric conduct', he died at Treassowe in 1823, aged 63; his funeral, held on 9 January, was attended by 5-6,000 people. An obituary notice in the *Royal Cornwall Gazette* described how he had parted from his wife after she permitted a relative, who was taking his leave on going abroad, to kiss her. He had also quarrelled with the clergyman of the parish over a charge levied for the erection of a tombstone on the grave of his two daughters, declaring that he would never be interred in the churchyard. James Hosking accordingly selected a spot on his own land at Castle-an-Dinas, enclosed a small space with a wall and fixed a tablet at each end, one bearing the inscription 'Custom is the idol of fools' and the other 'Virtue only consecrates the ground'.

According to another, more colourful version of the story, Hosking kissed the rector's wife, whereupon the gentleman vowed that he would bury the farmer in the most obscure corner of the graveyard, on the north side of the church; it was because of this that he determined to be interred with his family in unconsecrated ground. In January 1964 an extension to the large stone quarry at Castle-an-Dinas necessitated the removal of Mr Hosking's remains, with those of his eldest son and daughter, which were reinterred outside the ruins of the old chapel at Shillingham Manor, Saltash, the residence of his great-great-grandson, John Treffry Hosking.

131

LUDGVAN WESLEYAN PRAYER LEADERS' PLAN,
1840.

PLACES AND TIME.	MAY 31	JUNE 7	14	21	28	JULY 5	12	19	26	AUGUST 2	9	16	23	30	SEPTEMBER 6	13	20	27	OCTOBER 4	11	18	25	NOVEMBER 1	8	15	22
Trassoe, Sunday 2½	6	..	1	..	3	..	5	..	2	..	4	..	6	..	9	..	8	..	7	..	10	..	12	..	11	..
Long Rock, do. 2½	3	1	16	2	4	3	1	9	7	15	5	13	3	11	2	9	6	12	11	4	13	9	11	1	10	12
Varfell, do. 2½	4	..	12	..	16	..	2	..	3	..	7	..	4	..	5	..	10	..	1	..	6	..	8	..	9	..
Velianoweth, do. 2½	12	11	3	1	2	4	7	6	5	8	9	10	12	13	15	14	16	11	3	1	2	7	4	6	5	10
White Cross, do. 2½	..	5	..	15	..	11	..	14	..	1	..	8	..	9	..	2	..	3	..	6	..	5	..	4	..	..
Curewrian do. 2½	5	16	15	14	13	12	11	10	9	7	8	6	5	4	3	1	2	16	15	11	12	13	9	8	7	10
Church Town, Monday 7	15	2	1	3	5	4	7	6	11	9	10	8	15	11	13	16	12	2	1	3	5	4	7	6	8	9
Castle Gate, Do. 7	10	15	14	16	6	7	13	12	8	4	11	5	10	3	9	2	1	15	14	16	7	6	13	12	2	4
Trevorrow, Do. 7	1	9	11	13	15	14	16	8	7	10	3	2	1	4	5	6	9	11	12	11	10	13	15	16	7	8
White Cross, Tuesday 7	8	16	15	14	1	2	4	3	6	5	7	9	8	10	11	12	13	16	15	4	3	5	6	7	11	2
Trassoe, Do. 7	7	11	13	12	10	16	15	1	5	3	2	11	7	8	9	6	13	10	15	16	2	..	11	12	1	5
Long Rock, Do. 7	4	5	12	10	15	8	2	16	11	6	9	10	1	7	12	3	4	6	8	10	9	7	3	4	3	2
New Chapel, Thursday 7	13	1	2	4	3	5	6	9	10	8	12	7	13	15	16	11	14	1	2	5	4	3	10	8	6	12
Trenowin, Do. 7	11	3	1	2	7	6	8	5	14	13	15	12	11	10	5	3	9	16	14	8	11	1	2	13	15	16
New Town, Do. 7	3	2	5	7	9	12	14	13	12	11	6	4	3	2	1	8	15	5	9	7	13	12	11	10	16	1
Varfell, Friday 7	12	4	6	9	8	1	3	2	13	14	16	15	12	5	6	7	8	10	11	2	1	9	12	14	5	13
Old Chapel, Do. 7	2	8	7	6	5	3	9	11	1	2	6	8	1	2	14	13	10	1	5	6	11	1	7	9	8	16
Curewrian, Do. 7	6	13	10	11	16	15	12	7	1	2	4	3	6	9	5	10	11	12	13	5	6	15	16	3	4	5
Ludiesse, Do. 7	9	6	9	8	11	10	7	4	3	1	11	16	9	13	7	15	2	8	6	1	..	5	4	3	12	15

COMPANIES.

1 Taylor, Trythall, G. Trewren, May. R. Taylor, J. Pearce.
2 Leacher, Champion, S. Nicholls, R. Richards P. Semmens.
3 Hall, Ellis, J. Leacher, W. Hollow, Bryant, J. Chellew.
4 Trembath, Betty, Treorea, Chapel, Clark, R. Chellew.
5 Wills, Semmens, Thomas, Pooley, R. Roberts.
6 Nicholls, Johns, Allen, J. Johns, Trevaskis.
7 Payne, J. Hosking, T. Hosking, A. Nicholls, W. O. Williams. J. Phebey.
8 Blight, T. Johns, Catron, Rosewarne, H. D. Thomas.

9 Trewren, Roberts, Richards, Martin, J. Champion.
10 Morris, Searl, J. Lanyon, Barns, W. Nicholls, G. James.
11 Kenran, T. Martin, T. Catron, J. Hall, J. Ellis.
12 Williams, Carter, Z. Williams, H. Nicholls, Tonkin, H. Berriman.
13 Taylor, Pearce, J. Trewren, Berriman, J. Roberts, J. Martin.
14 R. V. Hosking, W. Hosking, W. Catron, Lanyon, Hollow.
15 Holman, R. Thomas, Rule, Z. Curnow, H. Thomas, S. Blight.
16 M. Thomas, J. Semmens, M. Chellew, E. Trevorrow, J. Trevorrow, R. Bawden.

The Prayer Leaders will meet on the First Sunday in every month, after Evening Service.

ABOVE: Ludgvan parish church. (CH, WT) BELOW: Ludgvan Wesleyan Prayer Leaders' Plan, 1840, found some years ago in the printing works of the *St Ives Times and Echo*. (M, WT)

Gulval

Gulval shares some of the characteristics of its near neighbour, Ludgvan. It too is divided into the low-lying Morrep and elevated Gundron, ranging from sea-level at the Eastern Green through rich farms and sheltered valleys to the higher cultivated areas, backed by bleak windswept moors at Mulfra and Castle-an-Dinas.

The high northern moors of the parish are the site of impressive antiquities, notably the Boskednan stone circle called the Nine Maidens, and the truly remarkable ancient village of Chysauster, with its street of circular beehive huts surrounded by an extensive system of garden terraces. It is believed to have been occupied by Iron Age people during the second or first century BC. Much lower down, at Bleu (Parish) Bridge, is a stone inscribed 'QUENATAU DINUI FILIUS'.

The identity of Gulval's patron saint is as uncertain as Ludgvan's. Mr Henderson remarks that the Celtic name of the Gulval church lands survives in the name of the manor house still adjoining the parish church: Lanisley, or properly, Laniskly. This was probably derived from a suppressed Cornish monastery or 'lan' and 'Escli', perhaps a personal name. The earliest known reference to the church's dedication to St Gulval was made in 1301, when the Jury of Penwith reported at the Eyre that John de Tregashyal (Tregaseal, in St Just) was taken for larceny and handed over to the Constables at Launceston, but escaped and took sanctuary in the Church of Sancta Welvela of Laneskly, where he abjured the realm. In 1413 the Bishop's Register referred to the church as St Gwelvela alias Welvela of Lanescly.

St Welvel has been identified, perhaps too hastily, with a Breton saint called Gudwal or Gurval; since Breton hagiographers are themselves undecided whether these names refer to one or two persons, and since no definite link can be established between him (or them) and the Cornish St Gulval, the matter remains clouded in uncertainty. St Gudwal was supposedly born about AD 500 in Wales, where he collected eighty-eight monks in a little island called Plecit. From there he passed by sea to Cornwall and Devonshire, and thence to Brittany, where he succeeded St Malo as bishop of that see. Canon Doble admitted that whether St Gudwal had anything to do with the Celtic monastery which must have existed at Gulval remains a moot point; 'If *Wolvella* be a different name from Gudwal, we can only say that nothing is known of St Wolvella'.

The mysterious Gulval left his mark on the parish in several ways, not least in providing it with Cornwall's most famous holy well. Says Hals: 'In Fosses Moor, part of the manor of Lanesly, in this parish, is that well-known fountain called Gulval Well. To which place great numbers of people, time out of mind, have resorted for pleasure and profit of their health, as the credulous country people do in these days, not only to drink the waters thereof, but to inquire after the life or death of their absent friends; where, being arrived, they demanded the question at the well, whether such a person, by name, be living, in health, sick, or dead; if the party be living, and in health, the still quiet water of the well-pit, as soon as the question is demanded, will instantly bubble or boil up as a pot, clear christaline water; if sick, foul and puddle waters; if the party be dead, it will neither bubble, boil up, or alter its colour or still motion. However, I can speak nothing of the truth of those supernatural facts from my own sight or experience, but write from the mouths of those who told me they had seen and proved the veracity thereof. Finally, it is a strong and courageous fountain of water, kept neat and clean by an old woman of the vicinity, to accommodate strangers for her own advantage, by blazing the virtues and divine qualities of those waters.' Sad to say, this well, near which there stood an oratory, subsequently declined so far in popular esteem that even its site — somewhere below the churchtown — is now uncertain.

The saint is also thought to be commemorated in the name of a farm in the higher region of the parish — Bosulval, in 1327 spelt Boswolvel, meaning 'the house of Gulval'. It was included with the rest of the parish in the manor of Lanisley, but no evidence exists of any ecclesiastical associations, chapel or holy well there.

Domesday Book states that Bishop Leofric held Landicle (Lanisley) before the Conquest, and that Rolland afterwards (1086) held it under the See of Exeter. The Beaupré family later had possession. Hals asserts that the manor, together with the advowson of the church, was given by his ancestor Simon de Als to the Augustinian Canons of St Germans Priory in 1266. But this seems improbable, for as early as 1245, William, son of Richard Fitz Yve, claimed the advowson from Godfrey the Prior, and the dispute was settled in the latter's favour by a duel fought in court by their champions. The priory enjoyed the great tithe until its dissolution in 1538.

There is thought to have been a mediaeval chapel at Trezelah, and in 1308 a leper hospital existed at a place called Glas on the low ground below Tolver, or at 'Glasney Green' near Long Rock. A round-headed cross survives at Rosemorran, while in 1885, the insertion of a window in the eastern wall of the parish church led to the discovery of an Anglo-Saxon cross embedded in the stonework. This now stands outside the south porch, and its presence has led to speculation (discussed by the Rev F. W. Warnes) about a possible 8th century Saxon settlement at Treneglos, with a Saxon church on the site of the chancel of the present building.

A few fragments remain of a cruciform Norman church on the sloping site overlooking Mount's Bay; a chancel was added in the 14th century. The massive 60 ft tower was completed in 1440, and is unusual in that the circular staircase reverses its direction from anti-clockwise to clockwise half way up. The entire outer wall of the south aisle was rebuilt and a porch added in the 16th century. Box pews and galleries came with the 18th century, only to be removed again in the 19th. In 1890 the collapse of part of the nave ceiling led to a decision to build the Bolitho Chapel and north aisle while the necessary roof repairs were being carried out; the 13th century north transept was demolished in September 1891. These alterations were effected during the incumbency of the Rev W. W. Wakefield, whose term of office lasted from 1839 to 1912, a total of 73 years. He first travelled down to Cornwall by stage coach; by the time he died, men had begun to master the air.

John Wesley preached near Gulval on Sunday 9 April 1744, and 'regulated' the Methodist Society already established here. His brother Charles preached at Gulval in the same year on Friday 27 July, and admitted some new members, 'particularly one who had been the greatest persecutor in all this country'. On 5 July 1745, as John Wesley was on his

134

way to Trezelah to preach, he was informed that the constables and churchwardens were come to oppose him, but found on arrival only 'a serious congregation ...After so many storms we now enjoyed calm, and praised God from the ground of the heart.' Altogether, six Methodist chapels were built at Gulval, most of which are now closed. The first chapel at Trevarrack was opened in 1822 and replaced by a larger one in 1884. Trezelah Chapel was demolished and removed piecemeal to St Ives, where it was re-erected in 1937 as the present Hellesveor Chapel.

In 1882-3 an unofficial 'Mission District' was established to serve the higher side of Gulval and Madron, in the charge of a curate licensed to Gulval. All Saints' Mission Church, at Trythall, was opened on 24 June 1885; rural depopulation led to the departure of the last curate in 1932, although the church itself continues in use.

Set amid the lonely moors in the north-west corner of the parish are the remains of one of Cornwall's most ancient mines, the celebrated Ding Dong which, if legend may be believed, furnished metal for the embellishment of King Solomon's temple. William Lemon, who married Isabel Vibert at Gulval on 22 April 1724, gained great wealth from the aptly-named Wheal Fortune in Ludgvan. He then moved to Truro, where he did much for the advancement of mining and succeeded in persuading Sir Robert Walpole to lift the tax on coal, which had been such a burden on the Cornish mine owners. His grandson, Sir William Lemon, was created a baronet in 1774 and represented Cornwall in Parliament for many years.

Kenegie, now a country club, was formerly the residence of the Harris family, one of whose members, Arthur, was Captain of St Michael's Mount in the 17th century. Judging from William Bottrell's collection of tales concerning the ghostly activities of Wild Harris and other spectres, Kenegie must have been one of the most haunted residences in England, but these ghosts are now still and have troubled no one for years past. Trevaylor was long occupied by the Veale family, which provided two vicars for Gulval. Beautifully named Rosemorran (vale of blackberries) was laid out by George John of Penzance during the early 19th century; he also created extensive plantations on the high moors at Try. The Bolitho family of Ponsandane, Trewidden and Trengwainton, by their active support of mercantile and productive enterprises such as mining, smelting, seine fishing, ship-owning and banking, created much employment to the benefit of all of West Cornwall. Their most memorable venture in Gulval was the smelting house at Chyandour. Though established by others before 1758, the works functioned most successfully under their direction throughout the 19th century, until its closure in 1912. The Prince Consort visited Chyandour in 1846 and dined on beefsteaks cooked on blocks of tin hot from the mould.

But Gulval's greatest economic asset has been its marvellous 'Golden Mile', extending along the lower side of the parish, where early potatoes, planted in November, have been lifted in April, while broccoli, cabbages and flowers can be grown with ease throughout the winter.

Today, the south-western corner of Gulval is being absorbed by the spreading conurbation of Penzance, with a heliport on the reclaimed Western Marsh, holiday chalets bordering the main road near Ponsandane, and housing developments at Pendrea, Vellanhoggan and Ridgeo. One hopes that the rural charm of this delightful parish with its pleasant valleys and rich acres of fertile land will not be too deeply eroded by modern needs, for such places are rare, and once lost can never be replaced.

ABOVE LEFT: Gulval parish ch
snr, then ten years old. (DM) INS
BELOW: Chyandour. (PHM) A
(DM, VTP) and BELOW: the C
Gulval cottage, demolished in
(DM) INSET: The Harris memo

e boy on the right is Ralph Corin
e 13th century font. (FWW, WT)
IGHT: Carriage folk at Gulval,
nily, photographed before their
en the churchyard was walled.
Gulval church. (FWW, WT)

137

ABOVE: The Old Inn (right) and Tregonning's cottage. (PHM) BELOW:
Penzance from Gulval, drawn by J. T. Blight.

138

ABOVE: The white buildings were barns used for temporary housing during the rebuilding of the village cottages in the 1890s. (DM) BELOW: Chyandour smelting works. (PHM)

ABOVE: Trevalyor, former home of the Veale family. (SSI) CENTRE: A train approaching Penzance station over the viaduct at Ponsandane. After being twice washed away by the sea, the viaduct was replaced by a stone embankment. (DM, G) BELOW: A meet in New Mill village. (DM, VTP)

St Michael's Mount & Marazion

St Michael's Mount, in any of its varied moods, always arrests the eye and quickens the imagination of the beholder. Its history is as rich and colourful as its appearance, extending back through the centuries into the dim mists of legend and romance. It is said that the island itself was built by Cormoran, the Cornish giant, with granite rocks brought by his wife Cormelian from Castle-an-Dinas, some miles distant. Noticing a greenstone rock nearby at Ludgvan, she placed it in her apron to save time, but Cormoran, meeting her on the causeway, gave her a kick for her laziness: her apron string broke and the rock rolled into the sea, to become what is now the Chapel Rock.

The Mount giant was troublesome to mainland dwellers because of his propensity for sheep stealing. So it was that Jack the Giant Killer decided to kill him by enticing the monster to chase him down the island slope where, falling into a pit concealed by branches and ferns, he fell an easy victim to Jack's club. The Mount has links with another famous story, for it was here that King Mark sent the hermit Ogrin to buy Isolde's wondrous raiment of many coloured silk, wool and linen.

The Mount has been conjecturally identified as Ictis, the island off the coast of Britain where, according to Diodorus Siculus, the inhabitants took their tin in wagons at low tide, to be shipped to Gaul and thence transported to Marseilles and Narbonnes by packhorses. This was in the first century AD. William of Worcester, writing in 1478, gave the Cornish name of the Mount as 'Karrik Luz en Kuz', the Hoar Rock in the Wood; and although Canon Taylor, in his well known book on St Michael's Mount, has sought to prove that this name properly belongs to the Mont St Michel in Normandy, the presence of a submerged forest off the shores of Mount's Bay remains an undoubted fact. Carbon-14 dating of sample tree trunks carried out by Sir Gavin de Beer at the British Museum (*Geographical Journal* June 1960) gives the time of their submergence as 1700 BC plus or minus 150 years, so the Mount has probably been an island since 2000 BC, much earlier than was previously accepted. If its Cornish name is genuine, then it must be the echo of an ancient folk memory indeed.

Throughout Europe, hilltops and other lofty eminences were often dedicated to St Michael, probably, as Davies Gilbert quaintly remarks, because the Archangel was universally painted with wings and therefore tacitly imagined to have birdlike habits. He is credited with at least one appearance at the Mount. A legend given in the early 15th century *Festial* of John Mirk of Littleshall, Shropshire, appears to be a variant of the story of the apparition of St Michael on Mount Gargano, involving a bishop and a stolen bull. 'He aperet also to another byschop, at a place that ys callet now Mychaell yn the mownt, yn Corneweyle, and bade hym go to a hullus [hill] top that ys ther, and thereas he fonde a bull tent wyth theues, ther he bade make a chyrche yn the worschyp of hym. But, for ther wer too roches [rocks], won on aythir syde the chyrche, that the werke myght not vp for hem [the

141

work might not be erected because of them], Saynt Mychaell bade a man, yn a night, goo thedyr and put away thes roches, and drede nothyng. Than zede thys man thedyr, and set to the roches his schuldyr, and bade hom, yn the name of God and Seynt Mychaell, sterte vttyr [move apart]; and so they dydden as moche as nede was.' (Early English Text Society edition, p258).

During the late fifth century, St Keyne came to the Mount on a pilgrimage as a consequence of the apparition of St Michael, while the Mount well (where Jack slew the Giant) was dedicated to another saint of this period, Cadoc, who had a chapel at Padstow.

St Michael's Mount entered recorded history in the reign of Edward the Confessor, when the manor of Truthwall, of which it was a part, was held by Brismar the Priest. William the Conqueror gave the island to his half-brother Robert, Count of Mortain. During the 12th century it came into the possession of the Benedictine Abbey of Mont St Michel, in Normandy, to which it bears such a remarkable resemblance. A church was built in 1135 by the Venerable Bernard, Abbot of Mont St Michel, and a priory established for a priest and twelve monks.

All alien priories, including St Michael's Mount, were confiscated by Henry V in 1414, and in 1423 Henry VI bestowed it on the newly-founded Bridgetine Syon Abbey in Middlesex, in part expiation of his grandfather's (Henry IV's) involvement in the murder of Richard II. Throughout the Middle Ages, the Mount was a great place of pilgrimage, its attractions including stones from the Holy Sepulchre and a portion of the girdle and some of the milk of the Blessed Virgin Mary.

Besides being a religious foundation, the Mount was a fortress, and as such witnessed some exciting events. It was seized by Henry de Pomeroy for Prince John during the latter's rebellion of 1193-4, while in the Wars of the Roses the Lancastrian Earl of Oxford and his followers gained entrance disguised as pilgrims and held the place successfully for several months. The commander of the beseiging army, Sir John Arundel, was killed on the beach near Marazion, thereby fulfilling a prophecy that he would die on the sea shore. Perkin Warbeck, the Pretender, left his wife at the Mount in 1497 before setting out on his ill-starred attempt to win the Crown. During the Prayer Book Rising in 1549, some of the king's adherents took refuge there, but it was seized by the governor, Sir Humphrey Arundel, on behalf of the rebels. This resulted in another seige and the execution of Arundel and other leaders at Tyburn soon afterwards.

On the dissolution of the monasteries in 1539, St Michael's Mount was seized by Henry VIII and held by the Crown for over half a century, tenants and 'captains' being appointed to manage it and the garrison. Sir Robert Cecil purchased the Mount from Elizabeth in 1599, and in 1640 the Cecil family sold it to Francis Basset of Tehidy. During the Civil War Sir Francis Basset greatly strengthened its defences on behalf of Charles I, but following the collapse of the Royalist cause in 1646, his son, Sir Arthur Basset, surrendered it without firing a shot.

Colonel John St Aubyn, a former Captain of the Mount, purchased it in 1659 from the Basset family, who had been impoverished by supporting the losing side in the war. A year later, the garrison was disbanded. His son, Sir John St Aubyn of Clowance, was created the first baronet, and this family has continued in residence to the present. In 1887 Sir John St Aubyn, MP, was made Baron St Levan; it was he who greatly enlarged the Castle between 1873 and 1878, the architect being J. Piers St Aubyn. In 1954 the Mount was handed over to the National Trust, together with a large endowment for its upkeep.

The stone causeway which gives access to the island from the mainland at low tide was built during the early 15th century, the Bishop of Exeter granting an indulgence to those who repented of their sins and contributed to its cost. The ancient quay of the little harbour was rebuilt by Sir John St Aubyn in 1726-7 and further improved in 1824. It was formerly busy with shipping, but has lost its trade to Penzance.

The pilgrims of former times have been replaced by the more numerous visitors who every summer thread their way over the narrow causeway to the little harbour and make the stiff ascent up the cobbled path to the Castle, to visit its ancient fortifications, the beautiful 14th century chapel built on the foundations of the earlier one destroyed by an earthquake in 1235, St Michael's Chair (actually an old lantern set upon the tower), the Chevy Chase Room with its 16th century plaster frieze of hunting scenes, the Priest's Chamber, Lady Chapel and other historic features. St Michael's Mount is a unique heritage and the jewel in Cornwall's crown.

Marazion, sometimes called Market Jew, acquired some importance in the Middle Ages as the final reception point for pilgrims on their way to the shrine at St Michael's Mount. Charles Henderson has asserted that the town was formed by the merging of two separate villages, Marghasbyan (Marghasbyghan — Little Market) and Marghas-dyou. The second name, with its many variants — Markesew, Marghisiou, Marghesyow, Marhas-dethyow and so on — has aroused conjectures that the place originated from the visits of Eastern traders to the Mount for tin. A more likely translation would be 'Thursday Market' as the local markets and fairs certainly played a vital part in establishing Marazion's prosperity.

Robert, Count of Mortain, confirmed to the Mount some of its lands and the right to a Thursday market, before bestowing it on the Abbey of Mont St Michel. In 1250, Richard, styled King of the Romans, the younger son of King John, granted and confirmed 'to the Prior of the blessed Michael in Cornwall and to his successors, that they may have and hold, and for ever possess, the three fairs and three markets on their own proper ground in Marchadyou near the Barn, which three fairs and three markets they have hitherto held, by the concession of our predecessors, Kings of England, in Marghesbigan, on ground belonging to others'. These fairs were held on the Feast and Morrow of mid-Lent, the Vigil, Feast and Morrow of St Michael in Tumba, and the Vigil, Feast and Morrow of St Michael the Archangel. The lord of the manor of Truthwall subsequently obtained the right to hold a market at Marazion on Mondays and a fair on the Eve, Day and Morrow of St Andrew. The mid-Lent fair took place at the western end of Marazion and the Michaelmas fair in the Long Barn at Trevenner (Vennefire). The latter survived into the present century, and at the time of its disappearance had been held continuously for nearly 700 years.

From as early as the fifth century AD, the people of Marazion crossed from the mainland, tides permitting, to worship and be buried on the Mount. With the emergence of the parochial system, Marazion was included in the parish of St Hilary, whose church lies two miles distant, so that both places of worship presented difficulties of access to the townspeople. As Marazion grew in size and population, the need for a local church became even more apparent; and on 22 March 1308/9, the townsmen of Markusyou obtained a licence to celebrate Divine Service in the Chapel of St Ermes in the parish of St Hilary on Mondays, Wednesdays and Fridays, without prejudice to the mother church, the rector and vicar of St Hilary assenting. St Hermes, the patron saint of this chapel, was a Roman martyr whose remains are at Renaix, in Belgium. The only other churches in this country dedicated to him are also in Cornwall: at St Erme and St Ervan.

The Bishop of Exeter often held ordinations for West Cornwall in the Chapel of St

Hermes at Marazion. In 1371 Bishop Brantyngham ordained nine men there on 28 August, the Feast of St Hermes. The earliest known chaplain of Marazion was Radulphus, in 1410. After the town had achieved corporate status in 1595, the Corporation nominated the curates, subject to approval by the vicar, an arrangement which sometimes led to friction between the two parties. The chapel eventually became ruinous, and was largely rebuilt around 1735; in 1861 this rather mean but picturesque building was finally pulled down and a new church erected on the site. The exterior is of granite and Tregonning Hill stone, the interior of cut Bath stone and the font of St Stephens' granite. Apse windows in the chancel were presented by Mr Cole (churchwarden), Mr Michell (the Mayor) and Piers St Aubyn (the architect), while the oaken lectern was given by the Vicar of St Hilary, the Rev Thomas Pascoe. The new chapel-of-ease to the mother church of St Hilary, called All Saints', was consecrated by Bishop Trower (acting for the Rev Henry Phillpotts, Lord Bishop of the Diocese of Exeter) on 24 June 1861. In 1892 Marazion was constituted a separate parish, the then curate, the Rev J. F. Lemon, becoming the first incumbent. An earlier curate of Marazion, Henry Francis Lyte, who served here from 1817-19, was the author of several well-known hymns, including *Abide with me;* the first two lines, with the familiar tune, are incorporated in the War Memorial railings opposite the church.

Leland, in 1538, referred to 'a lytle chapel yn the sand nere the towne toward the Mount'. Dedicated to the Blessed Virgin Mary, this stood beside the causeway on Chapel Rock. On 17 July 1645 Lord Hopton, at the command of Prince Charles, ordered 'the old decayed chapple upon the Rock to bee puld downe and the stone left lose upon the playne grounde of it'. Not a trace now remains of this building, which appears to have been erected during the early 15th century, since John Meger by his will of 1419 left 4d to the fabric of the newly-built chapel 'super lez Rokkes' near St Michael's Mount. On the causeway near the rock, the base of a stone cross destroyed by a storm around the year 1750 may still be seen. Another chapel, that of St Katherine 'in the parish of St Hilary next Markysyow', was licensed for Divine Service by Bishop Lacy on 26 April 1426.

The Friends' Meeting House, built in 1684 in Beacon Road, is the oldest public building in Marazion, and has lately been attractively restored and enlarged. Ebenezer Methodist Church dates from 1862 and the Fore Street Methodist Church from 1893, the latter replacing a late 18th century chapel.

The former importance of Marazion is reflected in the fact that during the reign of Henry II it sent two members to Parliament, but after the dissolution of the priory on the Mount, this privilege was forfeited through the town's inability to pay their wages. About the year 1513, it suffered a fate common among Cornish seaboard towns, when it was plundered and burnt by armed men who landed from thirty French ships of war. The town suffered further injury during the reign of Edward VI, this time from 'a multitude of Rebells and Enemies of the King'.

Marazion was granted a Charter of Incorporation by Elizabeth I in 1595, thus obtaining borough status some years earlier than Penzance and St Ives. By the charter, the town was to be governed by a mayor, eight burgesses or aldermen and twelve capital inhabitants. Its privileges included a weekly Saturday market and two fairs, one on the Feast of St Barnabas, the other being the confirmation of St Andrew's fair.

Unfortunately, the possession of a charter could not protect Marazion from the competition of Penzance, which began to develop from an obscure fishing village into a significant town, and during the 17th century, disputes arose between the two as a result of Penzance setting up an allegedly illegal market in opposition to Marazion's. The inhabitants of Marazion no doubt experienced some satisfaction when, in 1648, some of their men under Col Robert Bennett, who held St Michael's Mount for Parliament, suppressed a Royalist insurrection at Penzance, pillaging the town and taking forty prisoners, who were lodged in the 'Chappell of Marazion'. A 'new locke and kaye' were purchased for the door to make sure they did not escape.

A significant development in 1760 was the construction of a new turnpike road from Falmouth through Penryn and Helston to the bridge at the western end of Marazion, which also opened up a new approach from Penzance. In 1814 the Turnpike Trustees ordered 'Side Gates to be erected at a place called the High Lane, near Marazion Gate, also at the entrance of the Fair Court; and at Trevennah Lane; all the said roads adjoining the Helston Road'. Another means of communication was provided in 1852 with the opening of the West Cornwall Railway between Truro and Penzance; but Marazion station, inconveniently situated some distance from the town, is now little more than a memory.

Marazion was once the centre of an important mining area, extending mainly over the parishes of St Hilary and Perranuthnoe. A considerable fishing industry was carried on both at Marazion and St Michael's Mount, particularly pilchard seining, for which the shallow water was most suitable.

The 19th century witnessed the development of Penzance into the leading commercial centre of West Cornwall; Marazion, by contrast, lost first its markets and then its fairs, while shipping deserted its little quays for its rival's better port facilities. Eventually came the sad day in 1886 when Marazion was obliged, though not without a struggle, to relinquish its corporate status. During its 291 years' existence, the Corporation had acquired an impressive collection of records and beautiful regalia, comprising two small early maces (1595), two large silver maces (1769) and the silver-headed malacca cane presented in 1684 when Francis St Aubyn was Mayor. To safeguard these treasures, a Charitable Trust was established under the Charity Commissioners, which still functions, using income from properties and investments for projects of benefit to the town.

The last Mayor-choosing ceremony, held in October 1885, was a sad occasion. 'Before eleven o'clock in the forenoon', the Mayor, Thomas Lean, accompanied by the Town Clerk, T. Cornish, took their places in the Council Chamber, where, in accordance with ancient custom, the insignia of the Corporation were placed on the table, with the Charter of Queen Elizabeth I in the centre. Those present included Messrs A. O. Michell, J. Grigg, R. Michell and W. Pearce, burgesses, and T. Richards, R. C. Laity, J. Marks and R. Phillips, capital inhabitants. Mr Lean was unanimously re-elected Mayor, this being the eighth time the honour had been conferred on him. He was subsequently elected first Chairman of the Town Trust, an office he held until 1906. Mr Lean died in 1908, aged 82.

From 1886 until 1974, Marazion had a Parish Council under West Penwith Rural District Council; it has since been under the jurisdiction of Penwith District Council. By resolution, the Parish Council adopted the name of Marazion Town Council, the Chairman of which became the Town Mayor. In 1975 the Town Trust presented the Town Council with a beautiful solid silver badge of office, bearing the arms of Marghaisiewe, a castle signifying the Mount. The original Latin inscription (not used on the badge) ran: 'Sigill. majoris Ville et Borov. de Marghasiewe'. The centre of local government at Marazion is the Town Hall, which, with St Thomas' Hall, was built in 1870-1 on the site of the old Guild Hall and Market House.

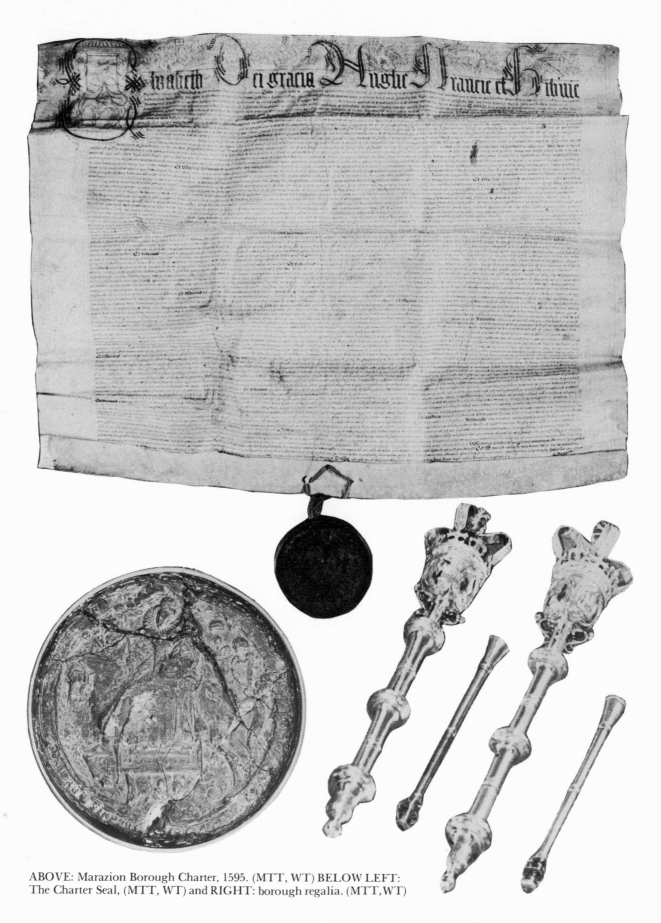

ABOVE: Marazion Borough Charter, 1595. (MTT, WT) BELOW LEFT: The Charter Seal, (MTT, WT) and RIGHT: borough regalia. (MTT, WT)

146

ABOVE: Marazion corporation accounts, 1815-1816. (MTT, WT)
BELOW: The Friends' Meeting House, Marazion. (WT)

147

MARAZION.

A PUBLIC MEETING

OF THE

RATE-PAYERS OF THE TOWNSHIP OF MARAZION,
Will be held in St. THOMAS'S HALL, Marazion,

On Tuesday next, March 9th,

At half-past Seven o'clock, in the Evening,

To take into consideration the Report of the Royal Commission on Municipal Corporations, lately issued, and if then so decided on, to adopt a Petition that this Township be placed in the position of the Boroughs included in Schedule B, of the Act of 1835, (5th & 6th, Will. IV, c. 76.), or otherwise.

Dated, 2nd March, 1880.

THOMAS LEAN,

MAYOR.

ABOVE: Marazion's efforts to retain its borough status in the 1880s are revealed by this poster. (MTT, WT) BELOW: The words and music of Henry Francis Lyte's hymn *Abide with me.* (WT)

ABOVE: The Godolphin Arms, (PHM) and BELOW: Turnpike Hill,
Marazion. (PHM)

149

ABOVE: Thomas Lean, last Borough Mayor, and T. H. Cornish, Town Clerk, with the borough regalia in 1880. (MTT) BELOW: Upper Fore Street, Marazion. (PHM)

150

ABOVE: The Prince and Princess of Wales land at St Michael's Mount in 1865, (ILN) and BELOW: the Mount with a train of the West Cornwall Railway, c1855.

151

ABOVE LEFT: Marazion Station, (R) and BELOW: the Marazion
Wesleyan Tea Treat on Treglown's picnic grounds, 1910. (R) RIGHT:
Lord St Levan's boatmen in traditional costume. (G)

Appendix I

A Mousehole Charter

'The King to the Archbishops, etc., greeting. Know that we have granted, and by this our charter confirmed, to our beloved and faithful Henry de Tyeys, that he and his heirs have for ever a market every week on Tuesday, in his town of Mosehole, in the county of Cornwall; and a fair there every year, to last three days, viz, on the eve and day and morrow of Saint Barnabas the Apostle (unless the market and fair injure neighbouring markets and fairs); and that they have free warren in all their demesnes of Alwerton in the same county, of Shireborn in Oxfordshire (provided these lands are not within the bounds of our forest) so that no one is to enter those lands, to hunt on them, or to take anything connected with the warren without the will and leave of Henry himself or his heirs, under a penalty to us of ten pounds. Wherefore we will, etc. Witnesses, the venerable father the Bishop of Wart. (?), John de Warenne Earl of Surrey, Henry de Lacy Earl of Lincoln, Thomas Earl of Lancaster, Hugh de Veer, John de St John, Hugh de Despenser, Robert Fitzwalter, John Botecourte, Walter de Beauchamp, John de Merks and others. Given by our hand at Holmcotram on the fifth day of September, by brief of privy seal.'

This Charter was granted in 1300 by King Edward I to Baron Henry de Tyes, Lord of the Manor of Alverton and of half of the Manor of Tywarnhail, who was summoned by writ to the House of Lords from 1299 until his death in 1308. He married Avice, by whom he had a son Henry. Avice died in 1326, seised of lands in Wiltshire. The son Henry being beheaded for treason in 1321, the manor of Alverton came to his sister Alice, then wife of Warine de L'Isle. It was that lady who in 1332 obtained from Edward III a Charter granting a market and fair at Penzance, with a seven day fair at Mousehole beginning on the Eve of St Bartholemew.

Appendix II

King Athelstan's Charter to St Buryan

'The Charter of Athelstan King of the English to the Church of St Berian in Cornwall.

The Kingdom of our Lord Jesus Christ endures, the ages of this world glide rapidly away, bearing, as flotsam upon their most swift current, kingdoms with their kings, which however reinforced as every wise man knows, sink from the level of their ancient standing, and the kings sigh for the joys of the life which is fading here.

Wherefore I, Athelstan, King of the English, as well as the Governor and Regent of the people living round about, have on the petition of my nobles granted a certain parcel of my land in the district named after the Church of St Berian: that is to say I have bountifully bestowed, in honour of God and the blessed Berian, for the redemption of my soul and the lengthening of my days to an eternal inheritance — one homestead divided into seven areas, with everything appurtenant thereto — fields, meadows, pastures, streams, fisheries, on the condition be it understood, that the aforesaid land is to be exempt from all secular assessment, but not from rendering of the prayers, which the Clergy have promised me, viz

100 Masses and 100 Psalters and prayers daily. If any man, however, should endeavour to come forward as a despoiler of this endowment, may his name be blotted out of the book of the living and not be written among the righteous. But for the man who stands as its steward and guardian, may God increase his days in the land of the living.

This aforesaid Endowment has been executed in the year dating from the Incarnation of our Lord Jesus Christ 943, 19 cycle 7, indication 2, concurrent 7, epact 12, of my reign 6, of the lunar cycle 5, the age of the moon 11, on the sixth day of October, in the town which is called Kingston. The aforesaid Land is bounded by these limits: viz: from the spring up to the ditch and from the ditch which is extended around Kescelcromleghe up to Yolbrunnemian and from thence to Fimbol and from thence up to Ponsprontiryon and from thence up to Mahenhalen and from thence up to Pelvagerens and from thence up to Mankependoun, going up the hill to Polmaduc and from thence round the ditch to Kacregan and thence along the direction of the road to the stream and going up-stream to the spring.

Next concerning the town which is called Bodenewel and has an area of three arpennae. The boundary of the township begins from Benberd and goes up the stream to Melynon and from thence up to Maentol in Lentrisideyn and goes along in the direction of the road up hill through the middle of Bosegham and thence in the direction of the ditch up to Fongad coming down between two ditches as far as the stream and from thence goes down as far as the sea.

In Pendre there is one arpenna; in Bokankeed there are three arpennae; in Botilwoen there are two arpennae; in Treikyn there are two arpennae; in Bosselynyn there is one arpenna and in Treverven there is one arpenna.

I, Athelstan, King of all Britain, have ratified this document with the seal of the holy Cross.

I, Hulshilmus, archbishop, have affirmed and signed.

I, Radulfus, archbishop, have assented and signed.

I, Donanus, bishop, have signed.

I, Ethelstanus, duke, witness.

I, Elsihe, duke, witness.

I, Beordolfe, duke, witness.

I, Hulfric, duke, witness.

I, Helfric, duke, witness.

I, Oddo, steward, witness.

I, Hulfil, in Trimsine, witness.

I, Helpine, steward, witness.

I, Elsnod, court officer, witness.

I, Hulfar, court officer, witness.

I, Elfnod, court officer, witness.

I, Elfrid, court officer, witness.

I, Beomod, court officer, witness.

I, Edulfe, court officer, witness.

I, Beordafe, witness.

I, Ethelmarche, witness.'

From *A Short History of St Buryan* (1953), by the Rev C. B. Crofts, Rector of St Buryan. (Exeter Epis. Reg. 1238 AD Vol. ii, fol. 25b.)

Select Bibliography & Sources

Anon, *Marazion and St Michael's Mount* (Royal Silver Jubilee booklet) 1977.
    Morvah Church: The Church of St Briget of Sweden, n.d.
    Madron Parish Church, n.d.
    The Church and Parish of Sancreed, n.d.

Anthony, G. H., *The Hayle, West Cornwall and Helston Railways*, 1968.

Barton, D. B., *A History of Tin Mining and Smelting in Cornwall*.

Beckerlegge, John J., *William Lovett, of Newlyn, The Cornish Social Reformer*, 1948.

Blight, J. T., *Churches of West Cornwall*, 1885. *A Week at the Land's End*, 1861.

Bottrell, William, *Traditions and Hearthside Stories of West Cornwall*, 1870, 1873, 1880.

Buller, Rev John, *Statistical Account of the Parish of St Just in Penwith*, 1842.

Chope, R. Pearse, *Early Tours in Devon and Cornwall*, 1918.

Courtney, J. S., *A Guide to Penzance*, 1845.

Coward, Edna Waters, *St Hilary, The Church on the Hill*, 1974.

Crofts, Rev C. B., MA, FSA, *A Short History of St Buryan*, 1953.

Dines, H.G., *The Metalliferous Mining Region of South-West England*, 1956.

Doble, Canon Gilbert H., MA, Various titles in the *Cornish Saints* series of booklets, published in the 1930s and 1940s.

Edmonds, Richard, *The Land's End District*, 1862.

Hencken, H. O'Neill, MA, PhD, FSA, Scot, *The Archaeology of Cornwall and Scilly*, 1932.

Henderson, Charles, *The Ecclesiastical Antiquities of the 109 Parishes of West Cornwall* (serialised in *The Journal of the Royal Institution of Cornwall*, commencing 1956).
    University Extension Lectures given at Penzance 1924-5 on the history of West Cornwall.
    The Cornish Church Guide, 1925.

Hitchens, A. H., *Ludgvan Parish Church*, n.d.

Hosking, James Martin, *To America and Back with James Hosking*, 1811, 1970.

Hudson, W. H., *The Land's End*, 1911.

Jasper, Rev David J. M., *St Just in Penwith Church Guide*, 1976.

J. B., *St Sennen Church*, 1954.

Jennings, Canon Henry R., *Historical Notes on Madron, Morvah and Penzance*, 1936.
    The Story of St Mary the Virgin, Penzance, n.d.

Lach-Szyrma, Rev W. S., MA, *Newlyn and its Pier*, 1884.
    History of Penzance, St Ives, etc., 1878.

Marsden, Rev R. E., *The Centenary of the Church of St John the Baptist, Pendeen*, 1952.

Matthews, J. H., *History of the Parishes of Saint Ives, Lelant, Towednack and Zennor*, 1892.

Millett, G. B., *Penzance: Past and Present*, 1876.

Mitchell, Susie, *Recollections of Lamorna, 1977.*

Nicholas, Edith M., *A Short Guide to St Just and Pendeen,* 1968.

Nicholas, G. M., *A Short Description of the Church of Saint Erth,* 1963.

Noall, Cyril, *Cornish Seines and Seiners,* 1972.

        Smuggling in Cornwall, 1971.

        Cornish Lights and Shipwrecks, 1968.

        Levant, 1970; *Botallack,* 1972; *The St Just Mining District,* 1973.

        The Book of St Ives, 1977.

Noall, Cyril, and Farr, Grahame, *Wreck and Rescue Round the Cornish Coast,* Vol II: *The Story of the Land's End Lifeboats,* 1965.

Pearce, John, *The Wesleys in Cornwall,* 1964.

Pender, Nettie M., *Mousehole,* 1977.

Physician, A, (Dr J. Ayrton Paris), *A Guide to the Mount's Bay,* 1824 ed.

Pool, P.A. S., MA, FSA, *The History of the Town and Borough of Penzance,* 1974.

Rees, Edgar A., *Old Penzance,* 1956.

Revill, Mrs W. G., *Gwinear,* 1959.

Rowe, Harry, *When Cuddan Roared,* 1962.

Taylor, Rev T., *St Michael's Mount,* 1932.

Thomas, Charles, MA, FSA, *Phillack Church,* 1961.

        Gwithian: Notes on the Church, Parish and St Gothian's Chapel, 1964.

Thomas, Charles, and Pool, Peter, MA, FSA, *The Principal Antiquities of the Land's End District,* 1968.

Vale, Edmund, *The Harveys of Hayle,* 1966.

Various, *Nancledra WI Scrapbook,* 1951.

Warnes, Rev F. W., *The Parish of Saint Gulval-in-Lanisley,* 1977.

Wells, Mary, *The Church of St Erth,* 1974.

Also, various county histories and topographies by Davies Gilbert, C. S. Gilbert, Lake, Dr William Borlase, Lysons, etc.

Old Cornwall Journal.

London Gazette.

Journal of the Royal Institution of Cornwall.

Files of the *Royal Cornwall Gazette, West Briton, Cornish Telegraph* and *Cornishman.*

KEY TO CAPTION CREDITS
(Two sets of initials indicate photographer first, copyright holder second.)

AE	Alfred Eddy	DT	David Thomas	P	Preston
ACG	A. C. Glover	FF	Francis Frith	PHM	Penlee House Museum
AO	Alfred Olds	FWW	Rev F. W. Warnes	PCT	Penzance Charter Trustees
BLB	British Library Board	G	Gibson	PQ	Percy Quick
BS	Brian Stevens	GBW	Rev G. B. Whittaker	R	Richards
CCL	Cornwall County Library, Redruth	GRW	Rev G. R. Wells	RHC	Rev R. H. Cadman
		HH	Dr H. Hynes	RJE	Rev R. J. Elford
CH	Rev Charles Hutton	ILN	*Illustrated London News*	RJM	Rev R. J. Mackenzie
CRO	County Record Office, Truro	JBDC	Canon J. B. D. Cotter	SAG	S. & A. Govier
		JJC	J. J. Churchward	SB	Sam Bennetts
CT	Prof. Charles Thomas	JMH	J. M. Hosking	SSI	Studio St Ives
DJMJ	Rev David J. M. Jasper	LEC	L. E. Comley	TF	Ted Ford
DM	Dick Matthews	M	St Ives Museum	VTP	Vaughan T. Paul
DRC	Dora R. Chirgwin & W. Chirgwin	MD	Major & Darker	WEC	W. E. Chapple
		MF	Rev Maurice Friggens	WR	Rev William Rowett
DRO	Devon Record Office	MTT	Marazion Town Trust	WT	William Thomas

157

Subscribers

ENDPAPERS: FRONT — A copy of Norden's *Description of Penwith Hundred* from his *Speculi Britanniae pars ... Cornwall*, 1728. (BLB)
BACK — Sheet XXXIII from the first edition of the Ordnance Survey of England. (BLB)